LIFE SPAN

Also by the author

The Home for Unwed Husbands

Wife With Knife
Winner of the Leapfrog Global Fiction Prize

Rough Translations
Winner of the Flannery O'Connor Award for Short Fiction

Creek Walk and Other Stories

Iron Shoes, A Novel

Bothered

All the Wrong Places
Winner of the Spokane Prize for Short Fiction

LIFE SPAN

*Impressions of a Lifetime Spent Crossing
and Recrossing the Golden Gate Bridge*

MOLLY GILES

Santa Rosa, CA

Edited by Peg Alford Pursell
Designed by Amit Dey
Cover design by Dowon Jung
Author portrait © Ralph Brott

Library of Congress Control Number: 2023950097
ISBN 978-1-7336619-9-7 (pbk) | 979-8-9877197-0-1 (ebook)

Published by WTAW Press
PO Box 2825
Santa Rosa, CA 95405
www.wtawpress.org

WTAW Press is a not-for-profit literary press. We are grateful for the assistance we receive from individual donors, public arts agencies, and private foundations.

To DB

1945

If I start to behave like a normal three-year-old girl, my father will let me sit in the front seat of the moving van with him. But I will have to crawl out from under the kitchen table, wash my hands and face, and stop snarling. He did not come back from The War to be attacked by a wild tiger. He doesn't like having his ankles nipped at. He doesn't like being growled at. He doesn't think it's funny.

"She's not used to you yet," my mother explains. She stands in the doorway holding my sister Bridget in her arms. "The only men she knows are the milkman, the iceman, and that mounted policeman she tries to follow down the block every morning."

"Can do?" my father asks, nudging me with the tip of his shoe.

I nod.

"Look slippy," he says. "I'm leaving in five."

I scrub the crayoned whiskers off my cheeks and scramble down the stairs after him. I do not need help getting into the van. I do not need help closing the door. "Slam it again," my father says, and, a minute later, slamming it himself, "Jesus." When I kneel to look out the window, he pushes me down onto the seat. "You don't get carsick, do you?"

I shake my head.

"Good-o." He lights a cigarette, starts the van, and turns the radio on to a baseball game.

I am too shy to look at him so I look out the window. Mommy is right. I am not used to him yet. Ever since he's come back from The War, things have been different. I can't sleep in Mommy's bed anymore; I have to sleep with my cousins and Bridget and they are all still in diapers; I can't talk at dinner or run up and down the hallway; I can't swim in the bathtub or hang off the banister. No one listens to my stories; no one looks at my art. "She's spoiled," my father says. "You've let her run wild."

Grrrr.

Still, there is something about him. When my father walks through the apartment, I follow behind, trying to put my own feet where his have been; if he turns around, I stop; when he starts to walk again, I start too. I sneak into his closet and press his Army jacket to my cheek, so warm and rough. When I'm alone in the bathroom I stick a finger in his shaving cream, lick it, and spit it out before I get caught.

"I'll give you three," he says, "to stop kicking the glove box."

I didn't know I was kicking the glove box! It's just that I have never sat this high up before. I have never seen so much of San Francisco—apartment houses and trees and cars and jeeps crowded with soldiers sitting on their duffle bags and old women walking their dogs down the sidewalks.

A bus passes and another little girl waves at me, but she is gone before I can wave back. Approaching the Golden Gate Bridge, I catch my breath; it is like entering a tall orange palace with no walls and no roof. Gulls swoop above us, gray fog swirls around us, boats sail below. My father points to a car with people leaning out the windows taking photographs. "Look at those idiots," he says, and, in the same breath, "I told you to sit down."

"No, you didn't."

"No, I didn't?" He laughs without making any sound. "Do you know those are the first words you've actually spoken to me?"

I take a long deep breath of his cigarette smoke. It tastes warm and burnt toasty and I like it. I like the way his big hands look on the steering wheel and I like the way he sings to himself underneath the chatter of the radio. I hear the baby's crib and Mommy's typewriter and my rocking chair clink and jangle from the back of the van. They are going to the new house in Sausalito where my father will start his new job at the stock exchange and my mother will start a new novel and I will start preschool. I stretch my arms up higher and lean back to look up as one by one the bridge towers overhead hug us and let us go.

1946

For my fourth birthday, I am allowed to invite a friend over, which makes Mommy laugh because I don't have any friends. That is not altogether true. I have Miss Buck, our upstairs neighbor when we lived in San Francisco. "All right," Mommy agrees, as she lifts the phone and waits for the operator. "I'll ask her. I just hope she doesn't have a heart attack and die on us." Miss Buck is eighty-two and has had one heart attack already, but I hope she doesn't die for a long time. She has curly brown hair and sunglasses and walks with a cane. We used to bake sugar cookies together up in her room, and make paper dolls; she spread the funny papers out on her rug and taught me to read them.

"She wants to come but she's not sure," Mommy says, hanging up the phone. "She needs to figure out how she's going to get over the bridge."

That bridge! That long orange stick that keeps Sausalito so far away from San Francisco! We have to cross that bridge any time we go to the zoo or the doctor or Sunday School. Daddy doesn't commute on it anymore; he takes the ferry to work. Granny comes over on the Grey-hound Bus.

"I suppose we'll have to pay for a cab," Mommy says, angry with me. "Miss Buck doesn't have any money."

Miss Buck arrives on the night of my birthday with my favorite book tucked into her black purse. She rubs my head like she used to, and she and my parents have highballs on the porch and talk about The War and the stock market. Miss Buck wants to know how Mommy's novel is coming along and Mommy says it's almost done. Daddy wants to know if Miss Buck knew a friend of his, Flynn Fasbinder, who used to teach at an elementary school in the city too, although, Daddy adds, that was probably after Miss Buck's time.

Bridget and I listen, yawning, sitting on the front steps and killing ants with our fingertips. Nora sleeps in the bassinet beside us and although Bridget pays no attention, I secretly make a face when Miss Buck says again what a beautiful baby Nora is.

We have cake and ice cream, and I open my birthday presents—a fake wristwatch, a new nightgown, some soap bubbles, a coloring book. Miss Buck hands me a soft package wrapped in tissue and when I open it, I see she has sewn me a doll. I say thank you at once, hiding my horror, for despite its pretty embroidered face and long yarn braids, I know the material this doll has been sewn from. I recognize the ribbed nylon fabric. I have seen it drying many times on Miss Buck's towel rack. This doll has been sewn out of an old pair of her underpants.

"What are you going to name her?" Mommy asks.

The names that come into my head are so terrible I clamp my lips shut. Panty. Poop. Pee Pee.

"She looks like a Ginny to me," Mommy says.

"Ginny," I repeat.

After dinner I stick Ginny face down behind my dresser and go in to say goodbye to Miss Buck. She is sitting on the porch with *The Counterpane Fairy* on her lap. I am too old for it now, but I nestle beside her as she reads, stopping to point out a word here and there, waiting for me to sound it out, coaxing me when I stumble. "Soon," she says, "you'll be able to read all by yourself." She closes the book and scratches my arms up and down like she used to; I rock against her and think about the sick boy in the book, and how the fairy who visits him lets him choose any square of his quilt he wants and then takes him on an adventure to that square, off to the Arctic on the sea-green square, off to a magic circus on the black-and-white square.

"They left some colors out, didn't they?" Miss Buck says.

I nod, and start to say my favorite word from the crayon box, "Flesh," but stop because it reminds me too much of poor Ginny, and I do not know what I am going to do about Ginny yet.

"Orange," Miss Buck says. "Now where can the counter-pane fairy take the little boy that is orange?"

The Golden Gate Bridge, I think. Take him there and burn it down.

1947

"I have it," Granny repeats. She again extends a dime, two nickels, and five pennies pinched in her beige cotton glove. Mommy, behind the wheel of the Hudson, bats the gloved hand back as we near the toll gate.

"You paid last time." The car sways over the dividing line to the right.

"I certainly did not," Granny says.

"Yes," Mommy says, digging for a twenty-five-cent piece through the open purse on her lap, "you did." The car sways over the dividing line to the left.

"I think I know what I did and did not do," Granny says. She reaches across Mommy to thrust the money toward the open window. Mommy slaps her back. Granny plants her elbow in Mommy's chest. Mommy backhands her. The coins from Granny's glove shoot across the dash; the coin from Mommy's purse rolls onto the floor. Our car lurches and brakes. The car behind us screeches to a stop. Two other cars honk. A man yells. We kids sink down in back.

"Now look what you've done," Granny scolds.

"Look what you've made me do," Mommy snaps.

My cousin Susan and I search our pockets. I have three pennies. Susan has a nickel. We roll down the back window and give the man in the toll booth our change. He waves it away, nods toward our mother and grandmother hugging each other, each of them weeping *Sorry Darling So Sorry* and says, "Just get them out of here."

1948

The bus to the city is full but that's all right, I don't need a seat, I can stand in the aisle, I don't even have to hold on, I can balance like a circus star, better than a circus star, the trick is to hold your hands at your sides and keep your toes pointing straight ahead and stare at one thing only without blinking and I stare at the dead head of the red fox biting its own tail on the lady's neck as we go around curve after curve and into the tunnel (don't breathe) and out toward the bridge and I do not fall down once though sometimes I teeter and have to grab the back of the lady's seat and she turns and frowns but the red fox whispers You're The Best.

1949

The Boys have broken the swings again, so I put Nora on the roundabout and push as hard as I can to give her a long spin. Bridget has already disappeared into the honeysuckle hedge with Jimmy. I would never go into the hedge but Bridget isn't afraid of anything—except The Coodie, who wakes her up at night and looks a little like Mommy. Bridget shows Jimmy her gogo and Jimmy shows her his peepee and sometimes he gives her a Life Saver and sometimes he doesn't.

I climb up the jungle gym, sit on the top, and look down at the playground. I can hear people on the tennis courts nearby and I can look over the fence to the Bardwells' rose garden and I can see straight down the row of dark cypress trees where the crows squawk. Far off in the distance there's the Sausalito harbor, a bright wedge of bay and sailboats, and when I hang from my knees upside down, the boats sail back and forth. Nora calls my name and for a while I pretend I don't hear her but finally I climb down, annoyed because she has another "butterfly" in her underpants which means I will have to change her, but before I can do that, The Boys stampede up, all of them, Stevie and Pete and Stuart and Bobby, grinning as they circle around us.

"Guess what this is?" Bobby thrusts a battered red shoe in my face.

I am too terrified to speak. I know I shouldn't be. The worst The Boys can do is set your hair on fire, like they tried to do to Judy before she grabbed the lighter and threw it away. The Boys never really have the snakes or spiders they say they are going to shove down your dress. But there are so many of them. And they are so fast.

Nora takes her thumb out of her mouth. "It's a shoe."

"A dead girl's shoe." Bobby presses his freckled face close to mine and lowers his voice. "This little girl was in a car accident on the Golden Gate Bridge, see, and her car was hit so hard this shoe flew off her foot and landed clear over here."

Bridget comes up, tugging at her waistband. "No, it didn't," she says.

"No, it didn't," Nora echoes.

"Oh yeah?" Bobby ignores my sisters, his widened eyes on mine. "See that stain? Know what that is? Blood! The little dead girl's blood. Want to lick it? Here. Want to try it on? It's your size."

"One shoe's no good," Bridget says calmly. "Where's the other one?"

"Shark ate it," Bobby breathes. "With the dead girl's foot inside." He thumps the shoe on top of my head, then he whoops and wheels away and the rest of The Boys follow him. Nora and Bridget go to pick the shoe up but I tug them back and when I stop shaking, I lead them home.

Later that night when I am in bed, I change it all into a story. In the story I am alone in the playground wearing a white cowgirl skirt with buckskin fringe and I am riding Trixie, my gold palomino. When Bobby runs up with the shoe I see at once he doesn't know it is really a grenade that could kill him so I lasso it out of his hand with a flick of my silver lariat and scoop him up and put him behind me on the saddle and we ride swiftly away, explosions behind us. Bobby's arms cling to me as we ride. I love you, he says, I love you.

1950

"You're getting fat as a pig!" Mommy snatches the cookie out of my hand and takes my Oz book away. "She didn't use to be this fat," she explains to Denorah, who is standing in the corner of the kitchen ironing. "But ever since her best friend—what am I saying—her *only* friend, Judy, moved away, all she does is eat and read. I don't know what to do with her. God." She thrusts a hand into her hair and closes her eyes. "How am I ever going to get this novel written."

Denorah, silent, sprinkles water on a pillowcase and continues to iron. Mommy's eyes spring open.

"Go play," she orders me. "Get outside. Run. Jump. *Do* something."

Slowly, I go outside, sit down on the stoop, pull some grass up and eat it. There is nothing growing in the yard I haven't eaten: geraniums, oxalis, pine needles, rose hips. I am hungry all the time. Ants are bitter as black pepper; sow bugs crunch; melted tar on the street tastes like licorice. Except for the hiss of the iron and the sound of Mommy typing downstairs, the house behind me is quiet. Bridget is playing at Jimmy's house, Nora and Baby Danny are taking naps. This is Mommy's time to write her second book. Judy and I used to spend this time together working on our tree fort in the playground. With a sigh, I head for the fort to see if any of our tools are still hidden in the branches.

I am halfway up the hill when I hear a familiar whoop.

Not good. Johnny Pomeroy and Todd Sweet are behind me on their bikes. Todd is ten and says fuck. Johnny is a rich boy who is so dumb he brags about his father's yacht and three car garage at school. Yesterday when two older boys started to push him around at recess, I couldn't help myself and shouted, "Leave him alone!" Everyone stared and I blushed. I don't want anyone to know I think about Johnny at night.

"Fattycake, Fattycake," Todd singsongs, coming closer on his bike, and Johnny, of course, no spine, no brains, echoes, "Fattycake."

It isn't far to the tree fort now, and once I get there, I can escape but as I start to run, Todd growls, "Get her!" Johnny rams his bike straight into me. He knocks me down to the pavement. He wheels around and both he and Todd ride off fast in the opposite direction.

When I try to stand up, a bone in my leg jumps out against my skin so scarily that I can't look at it. I pull my skirt down and prop my head on my hand and lie there. The pain is sickening, and though I gag a little I do not throw up. The afternoon passes. I move bits of glass and gravel around with my finger and whisper, "Help" to a bush of berries that have already started to turn gold for Halloween. Cars pass but no one stops. Finally, a neighbor I know slows and unrolls her window.

"Are you all right?" she asks.

"Would you get my father?" I try to smile but that's when the tears come. "I really want my father."

The neighbor turns around and heads back in the direction of our house. I wipe my eyes. I'll be all right once Daddy comes. Daddy always knows what to do—he knows everything. I wave with relief as he drives up and parks, but he doesn't wave back.

"What did you do now?" he asks, standing over me.

"Nothing!" The tears fall fast now. "I didn't do anything! Todd and Johnny were chasing me on their bikes and Johnny ran over me."

"Johnny who?"

"Pomeroy."

"Pomeroy," Daddy repeats. "God." He bends down to pick me up. "So, what did you do to make him hit you?"

"Nothing!" I repeat. "I tried to run away!"

"You tried to run away?" Daddy groans as he lifts me. "How much do you weigh, anyway?" He drops me into the back seat of the car and leans over me. "Don't you know," he says, his voice cold, "that if you don't run, no one can chase you?"

The doctor comes to the house, says I have a broken shin and will have to go to St. Mary's Hospital in the city for a cast. He stays to have a quick drink with my parents and the neighbor and they all agree there is no sense involving the Pomeroys; it was just an accident, an accident that wouldn't have happened if I wasn't so fat. Daddy complains about his back and the doctor says he should have it looked at as well. Picking up someone as heavy as me might have sprained it. Mommy bends over me and smooths my hair. "We'll put you on a diet when you come home," she promises.

The neighbor stays to watch my brother and sister, and my parents, as merry as if they are going to a party, drive me to the hospital. I lie in the back of the Studebaker, alert with pain, staring up at the yellow lights of the bridge as we pass under them on our way to the city.

If you don't run, no one can chase you, I repeat to myself. *If you don't run, no one can chase you.* I see the logic. The words make perfect sense. Daddy is right. And he is wrong. Wrong wrong wrong.

At the hospital, my leg is put in warm heavy plaster; I am told I'll be fine and given a bed for the night. I am not yet asleep when a man I haven't seen before comes in. He draws a curtain around us, pulls on a plastic glove, says, "This is standard procedure, so don't make a fuss," parts my thighs and inserts his finger deep into my center. I am too shocked to move; it is as if he has reached inside and pinched my secret heart, hard. The man's face is expressionless, his eyes set on something far away. After a while he pulls his finger out, peels off his glove, puts it in his pocket, and leaves without saying goodbye. There is no need for him to warn me not to tell anyone. There is no way I ever would. And anyway, there is no one to tell.

1951

Mommy lights a cigarette and hands it to Daddy, who is driving, and then lights another for herself and exhales. Her lipstick smells like red roses; the four of us can smell it even here, in the back seat. Nora touches my knee. I raise my voice. "Nora's going to throw up," I announce.

"She can't." Mommy does not turn around. "We're on the bridge. We can't stop on the bridge. She'll just have to wait until we get home."

Home is Mill Valley and Mill Valley is two hills and a tunnel away.

Nora gags.

"She can't wait," I say.

"Get the can." Mommy sighs.

I reach under the seat, pull out the Hills Brothers coffee can with the picture of the old man in his yellow nightgown on the front, and hold it under Nora's chin. "Don't get any on me or I'll kill you," I whisper. Nora leans forward, gags again, and heaves. I look away. The can gets warm and heavy in my hand. I can't hold my nose but I can breathe through my mouth and my mouth fills with the stench of sour milk, sour Cheerios, sour oranges plus red roses cigarette smoke coffee dust and tin, and so must the mouths of Bridget and Danny, who both say, "I feel sick, too," but not before Nora vomits again.

1952

Mrs. Tether goes to the blackboard. "Describe the bridge in the fog," she writes. Okay. I open my notebook. I can do that. *A dragon in a bubble bath.* "That's good," Mrs. Tether says, "I can tell you are going to be a writer like your mother," and she reads it out loud to the class and I open the lid of my desk and put my head inside, blushing. I want more than anything to be a writer. Mommy wrote one book; she has not finished another, but once a year she gets dressed in her gray fox stole and her silk dress and drives to the city to have martinis with her agent at the St. Francis Hotel. When she comes home, she is flushed and gay and wants us all to dance with her, although later we can hear her crying in the bedroom.

Mrs. Tether continues to collect our notebooks and reads the next one by Alice Churchill, which is something dumb about strawberry popsicle sticks spelling big H's in the sky. "Another budding writer!" Mrs. Tether says. "Very imaginative!" She asks us all to clap for Alice, which I only pretend to do, with my head still down and my hands in my lap.

1953

Whenever Great Aunt Ethel and Great Uncle Will visit, Bridget and I have to go to The First Church of Christ Scientist in San Francisco with them. We don't mind; we get a lot of attention there and sometimes we even get lunch in the city. Since Great Aunt Ethel is a Practitioner, we are mobbed by old ladies after the service. Bridget is praised for her blonde curls and I am admired for the faraway look in my eyes during The Lesson.

"What part of *Key to The Scriptures* were you thinking about?" I'm asked. Wisely, I say nothing, because of course I had been thinking about the extra quarter tucked inside my glove, which I had not offered during The Collection, and about what the fat soprano would look like stripped bare naked.

I had also been savoring something I had heard Granny say about Great Aunt Ethel that morning. It seems Great Aunt Ethel's marriage (her third) to Will was a puzzle. Will had been married previously to her late sister. "So, Will *knows* Ethel," Granny had marveled, and I in turn had marveled— Granny had said so much in so few words.

Great Aunt Ethel watches me now as I prod Bridget out the doors of the church, up the sidewalk, and into the back seat of Great Uncle Will's shiny black car. I want to ask about lunch—will we go to a restaurant or go straight home, but I don't dare; Great Aunt Ethel will understand at once that the "faraway look" in my eyes was false.

"Matthew 7:12," she says, turning in her seat, lifting the veil off her hat and staring at me.

"Yes?" I stammer.

"Yes?" she repeats, waiting.

"The Golden Rule?"

"Which is?"

"Do unto others as you would have them do unto you?"

"And to be merciful, just, and pure," Great Aunt Ethel finishes. She smacks her lips and settles back as Great Uncle Will drives us down the hill, out of the city, and toward the bridge.

So, no lunch at a restaurant today. Bridget starts to hum a hymn, the little brat. I turn to the window. The car in the lane beside us is full of lucky laughing children and I invisibly transport myself into their midst. As they pull ahead of us though, I see that the back tire on their car is wobbling and about to come loose. Alarmed, I lean forward.

"That car is going to lose a wheel," I say. "We should warn them." I roll my window down to shout out to the driver, but Great Uncle Will speeds up and passes them and Great Aunt Ethel tells me to sit down and roll the window up at once.

"That car is full of Southern Immigrants," she explains.

I wait, puzzled.

"Negroes. Don't worry about them. They can take care of themselves."

What would I do if I were merciful, just, and pure? Wouldn't I defy my aunt and shout a warning out the window anyway? Wouldn't I do unto others? Cowed by her hard gray stare, I say nothing and slink back, feeling new shadows of shame darken inside me.

1954

Nell's mother is a writer too, and Nell's house is almost as full of books as ours is, though her house is smaller and chillier and darker and has even less furniture than ours. Nell's younger sister and brothers lie on the floor and read the comic pages that, thickly spread, act as a rug, and Nell and I curl up in Army blankets and read the *Anne of Green Gables* books. We have made a map of Avonlea and pretend we live there. Sometimes one or two of her brothers play along with us, or her sister helps us make costumes. I cannot get over how affectionate this family is!

Bridget and I fight every night after dinner when we are supposed to be doing the dishes; we close the door to the kitchen and wrestle each other to the linoleum floor silently, not wanting our parents to hear. Danny and Nora fight all the time too. When Nora goes upstairs, Danny grabs her ankles and pulls her down on her stomach and when she kicks him in the face, he runs to get the bullwhip Mom and Dad brought him back from Mexico. "Stand still so I can hit you!" he yells but Nora, wisely, is long gone by then.

Nell's siblings share the one bicycle and split the last cupcake; they sit on their mother's lap and run to the door to greet their father when he comes home from his job as a longshoreman. I am fascinated, envious, and just a little repelled by their excitement as they cluster around him, chatting and laughing.

Sandra's family makes more sense to me. Sandra lives in a sunny ranch house with yellow walls. Her mother is expecting again, her father sells insurance, her younger sister takes tap dancing lessons, and her brother is in Little League. There is not a book in her house. At Sandra's I play tetherball and eat potato chips and watch *Your Hit Parade* on their television. We both are in Campfire Girls and go door-to-door selling mints, hoping to earn enough honor beads to sew onto our felt vests. At the roller-skating party we choose to be each other's partner; we go round and round, and when the lights go down Sandra pretends I am Gunther and I pretend she is Pat Boone. Mommy says I see too much of her; she says if Sandra jumped off the Golden Gate Bridge I probably would too, but Sandra would never do anything that stupid. Nell would. But I don't play with Nell anymore.

1955

Back on the bus again, squinched near the window with my Kotex belt digging into my groin while the woman beside me lifts her skirt to scratch a thigh oozing with poison oak and a strange man behind me reaches through the space between the seats to stroke my elbow, once, before I yank it away. People are ugly and awful and I hate all of them. If there were a button to push, I would eject everyone onto the pavement.

The bus stops to pick up a passenger and my old fifth grade teacher gets on. I stare straight ahead. There is no need to greet her. Years have passed. She will never recognize me. I am tall now and my curls have all been cut off to a DA. My pimples are hidden under a thick plaster of Clearasil, and although my eyes are still red from my fight with my mother, my lashes are heavy with the Maybelline mascara I swiped on after I slammed the door and left the house. My chewed fingernails shine with Revlon's Powder Pink. I clench the copy of *Lord of the Flies* on my lap, and stare out the window.

"Hello!" Mrs. Tether touches my shoulder as she passes. "How nice to see you, dear. You haven't changed a bit."

1956

"I don't like the way you're driving," Aunt Jean says to Mother.

"Fine," Mother says. "You drive."

"I should," Aunt Jean agrees. "At least I know how to hold my liquor. Susan," she says to my cousin. "Would you like to take the wheel?"

"Susan?" Mother yelps (only she says Shusan). "Shusan is fifteen years old and does not have her license."

"I can drive," Susan says quietly.

"Oh for god's sake." Mother wrenches the wheel sideways, zips across two lanes of the bridge approach, turns into the parking lot below the Round House Café, and brakes. Aunt Jean is the only one who has not screamed. "I'll get a cup of nice black coffee here, all right? Girls? You'd like a Coke, wouldn't you? Let's go inside. Happy?" she says to Aunt Jean.

"You almost killed us," says Aunt Jean.

"Well, but I didn't," Mother says. "Did I?"

1957

My friend Katie has driven through Toll Booth 3 six times already this week and today she has added "I am almost 18" below her name and phone number just to make sure Clem Mathis understands. Clem Mathis is Johnny Mathis' brother, she tells us, only better looking, and Katie definitely felt him press her palm with his thumb when he took her twenty-five cents in pennies yesterday and if the cars behind her hadn't kept on honking, she is pretty sure he would have asked her out. Diane and I can come to the toll booth with her this once but we have to shut up and not giggle like idiots, because Katie has never felt about anyone the way she feels about Clem Mathis and once he gets to know her, he'll feel the same.

"But you won't be eighteen for another two years," Diane points out.

"I said 'almost,' didn't I?" Katie checks her makeup in the rearview mirror. We are all wearing a lot of makeup and Diane and I have stuffed pieces of foam rubber from an old couch pillow into our brassieres, but so far it seems the only men who notice us are our fathers, who pinch our jaws and tell us to go wash the goop off.

Diane's sharp nails dig into my arm with excitement as we approach the toll booth and then retract when the woman taking Katie's pennies says Clem doesn't work today and no, she doesn't know when he'll be back. For a minute, I half expect Katie to start crying, but she just mutters, "If at first you don't succeed," makes a neat, quick, illegal U-turn and drives us back to Marin.

1958

"I'm sorry, dear," the nun on the bus seat beside me says, "are you praying?"

"No, oh, oops, sorry," I say. "I'm just practicing. I have to memorize this story for my drama class."

"What story?"

"It's called 'A Telephone Call'? By Dorothy Parker? I have to recite it by heart."

"What's the story about?"

"It's about this woman waiting for a man to call her. She sort of goes to pieces while she waits."

"Why did you choose it?"

"I thought it was funny."

"Is it funny?"

"No, it's actually sad. The woman is so miserable."

"Let's hear it."

"I can't. I don't really know it yet. I'm just learning. Plus, it's awfully long. "

"Well, just the beginning, then? Are you shy? You'll never get anywhere as an actress if you're shy."

"I don't want to be an actress."

"What do you want to be?"

"I want to be a writer."

"Like Dorothy Parker?"

"Yes."

"Someone who writes about sad miserable women who sit around waiting for gentlemen to phone them? Well good luck to you, dear. This is my stop. I will pray for you."

1959

Dan smells like Aqua Velva and Marlboros and I smell like Arpège and Tareytons. We pass a plastic cup of my parents' whiskey mixed with his parents' Scotch back and forth as we drive. My head is on his shoulder; I help him shift; he's such a good driver he can steer the Ranchero with his knees. We have never seen each other dressed up before, but this is surely how we're meant to look from now on: he like Peter Gunn in his dark suit, me like Kim Novak in my strapless lavender gown with my hair done up in a French twist. After the prom we are going to the Tonga Room and after the Tonga Room we are going to not-go-all-the-way under the bridge at Fort Point. I have not been this happy since I was a baby. I will write a poem about the city, the way the lights look like jewels on velvet, no, sequins on slate, no, diamonds on a pet jaguar's back, but I will have to write it later, for there is nothing in my purse but lipstick and a dollar, no pen, no paper. Dan turns the radio up—our song—André Previn, "Like Young"—and blows a perfect smoke ring and I poke through the center with my index finger like I always do and we both laugh as we cross over our bridge into our city.

1960

Our eighteenth birthdays are five days apart and as a gift my mother has bought tickets for Dan and me to see *Sweet Bird of Youth* at the Curran. My mother does not know that we are about to break up. We have broken up twice before and she never knew about those times either. She thinks Dan is "a nice boy," and before we leave for the city, she sidles in from the kitchen in her terrible plaid Bermuda shorts and orthopedic shoes to ask him if he recognizes this leaf she found in the garden; she has never seen a leaf like it before but perhaps he can explain it to her? He must be learning so much in his Botany Class at the JC! My father snorts from his armchair and cracks the newspaper open. Bridget and Nora make faces at me behind Dan's back and Danny follows us out to the curb; he admires Dan's yellow Ford convertible and hopes to be invited to ride it in someday. Once in the car, Dan gives me his birthday present, a carton of Marlboros, and I try to smile as I unwrap it, but I am hurt, thinking of the two Miles Davis albums I gave him and the love poem I wrote that he still has not mentioned. We go to dinner at Julius' Castle before the play and when the waitress comes with the check Dan pulls a one-hundred-dollar bill out of his wallet and snaps it back and forth before flipping it onto the tray. I close my eyes. So, this is why my father calls him The Jerk.

We go on to the theater and watch the actress drift across the stage in a sheer clingy nightgown. Geraldine Page is old and not beautiful but she is definitely naked under that gown. I glance at The Jerk's crotch in the dark to see if he has an erection. I cannot tell. I have not slept with him yet but I am sure that after tonight I never will.

Or at least not until I am nineteen.

1961

The doctor my roommate recommended has her office on Nob Hill in San Francisco. She is Japanese but somehow, with her gray hair, mottled cheeks, and warm brown eyes, she looks so much like my grandmother I start to stammer. She is concerned and kind. She talks to me about the test results. What I feared most is a fact. The baby is two months along and will be due in May. The doctor asks what year I am at Berkeley and what I am studying.

"Your education is the most important thing," she advises, her voice serious. "Take a semester off, go away, give the baby up for adoption and get back to the university."

I nod. I wish I could do that. I wish I were that kind of girl. Someone resilient and brave and honorable. A girl as the doctor herself must have been as a girl. But I am a sloppy student with peroxided hair and black eyeliner who smokes, swears, drinks too much, and draws daisies on her physics exams. One of my professors introduced me to a famous poet in the hopes the poet would work with me outside class, but the poet was busy grading papers and said he didn't have time for freshmen. A teaching assistant I admired said I had no business being in college in the first place; blondes like me should marry, he said, and stay at home. Some of my sorority sisters have already done just that; my best friend flunked out and another went to Mexico for an abortion, returned somehow still pregnant, and had to get married anyway.

I thank the doctor and resist the urge to lay my head against her shoulder. It's raining outside and I am wearing the trench coat, black turtleneck, and sunglasses I planned to wear in Vienna, when I became a foreign correspondent, wrote for *Time* magazine, had a thousand lovers, and traveled all over the world on secret assignments. I shake the doctor's small, strong hand and leave with my roommate, who's been waiting outside.

We drive back across the bridge in her Singer in silence. My roommate gets an allowance from her wealthy father and would probably lend me the five hundred dollars for an abortion, but she doesn't offer and I don't ask. We smoke and listen to a jazz station on the radio. I know I have to protect and guard the life inside me. I just don't want to.

I stub out my cigarette. I have already told Dan, and Dan, after saying, "Well I'm glad it's you and not someone else," asked only two things: that I stop shoplifting after we're married and that I never say fuck in front of the baby. I still have to tell my father. Oh god, my father. His thousand disappointments in me, compounded. Do I have to tell my father? Does he have to know?

My roommate pats my hand. "Can I come to the wedding?" she asks.

1962

Babs and Boyce are wealthy friends of Dan's parents and because Dan and I have no furniture and because they feel sorry for us, for our rushed Reno wedding, they have offered to drive us, "the kids" as they call us, across the bridge to a discount warehouse in South San Francisco they know and like. They have given us one hundred dollars to spend and they and their fluffy little Pekingese have followed us around as we've picked out a 9x12 rug of woven green seagrass, two iron butterfly chairs with blue canvas covers, an Indian print bedspread, a framed Van Gogh print of sunflowers, and a pole lamp. These, Babs says, will be delivered to our duplex by the next day and in the meantime they will drive us back to Mill Valley for hamburgers and milkshakes—we do like hamburgers and milkshakes?—and Dan and I say yes thanks we practically live off them—which we pretty much do, as I only know how to cook scrambled eggs and chocolate chip cookies, and we sink into the back seat of the Mercedes, and even with both our wedding rings resting on top of my huge swollen belly I feel exactly like what we've been called: kids.

1963

Gretchen sleeps in the infant seat beside me. She is seven months old. She does not know that it took me five permits to get my driver's license nor that I've only had it for two weeks. She does not know that I have never driven over the bridge before. She does not know the lanes are too narrow. She does not know the other cars are going too fast. She doesn't fear the proximity of the guardrail or expect the towers to crumble or the girders to buckle or the pavement to break in midair like a plank sawed in half and send us roaring into the ocean below. She does not know the fare has slipped from my fingers but she feels the bump as I brake and fumble for it and firmly rear-end the car stopped in front of us at the toll booth. She feels that all right.

Her blue eyes open and she stares at me, alert. She doesn't cry. She doesn't have to. I hear her question clearly. So this, she asks, is who I'm stuck with?

1964

Downpour. The window washers on Dan's parents' Lincoln Town Car can't go fast enough; there's no clear space; nothing to see; we are commuting home from the city inch by inch, blind and buffeted by heavy winds. Brake lights recede in front of us; headlights shoot up behind. The roar of the rain is horrific. I slump in the back seat, head down, the wife they never would have chosen for their son, trying to thread yards of shiny brown plastic Dictaphone tape back into the reel I broke on my third day at work. My fingers fumble, the slick tape tangles. I will lose this job Dan's father found for me. I will have to look for another. Unless we crash. I wouldn't mind if we crashed. I am about to wad the entire mess up and shove it into my purse when the sky above us suddenly clears and Dan's mother turns with her beautiful smile, holds out her hand, and says, "Here. Let me help you."

1965

But Marty was a joke! The way he shouted "Stella" in class and pretended to rip his T-shirt on stage. The theater sets he painted: clowns. He painted white-faced red-nosed yellow-wigged clowns! When he sat down on that stool with his guitar and began to sing with his high, strangely catlike voice, didn't we all cringe? All that emotion in that brokenhearted tremor! Any of it real? Yet here he is—Marty!—singing on the radio as I drive across the bridge to meet my old college roommate in North Beach. He sounds good. He sounds beautiful. There is nothing I can do but turn the song up and listen hard and wish I could sing along with him. But how can I? I can't carry a tune. I can't write a love song. I'm nothing but a suburban housewife who writes poems that no one will publish. I'm married to an insurance adjustor! We have no money! And I'm pregnant again! And this ex-roommate I am driving to see? Graduated with honors, married, divorced, childless, works in a publishing house in New York, and is having an affair with a married heart surgeon who takes her to Paris. How can I possibly spend all afternoon listening to her?

1966

Dan doesn't like to talk when he drives. But then Dan doesn't like to talk when he's not driving. Usually, I nag him about this. But today I don't mind. I have our new daughter to talk to. She lies on my lap as Dan drives us home from the hospital. She is not as beautiful as Gretchen was but she has a quality I somehow recognize, as if I have known her longer than these last two days. We have named her Rachel, after my grandmother, and she is swaddled in a blanket Granny knit for her, soft yellow wool. I have wished a long rich interesting life for Rachel, full of adventure, a life unlike mine. You will see the world, I say to her, you will travel. I bend close. You will know many languages, I promise. You will encounter wonders. Rachel looks past me, up at the clouds, her brown eyes unblinking.

In the back seat, Gretchen sings softly. Gretchen is four; she knows every word to our Beatles albums and can pronounce each of them perfectly, but in the hospital this morning she suddenly dropped to all fours and started to crawl and right now she has reverted to baby talk. "Dadababa," she sings, the only sound in our speeding car. I turn to her, smile. "Can you say Rachel?"

Gretchen plugs her thumb into her mouth and closes her eyes. No. She cannot say Rachel. Will not. Should not be asked to.

1967

Even sober, Mother is a terrible driver, slow and reckless. She resents these trips to see my grandmother in the rest home and won't do them at all unless I come with her. "She's always been willful," Mother says as she scrapes close to the curb in the right-hand lane of the bridge. "She never took care of herself; it's no wonder she's gone batty."

"Granny's not batty," I protest. "She's old."

"She's manipulative," Mother says. She speeds up to tailgate a truck.

"Manipulative?" I challenge. "Because?"

Because last week Granny got up at three in the morning, put on her silk dress, her beige coat, her brown hat, and sat down in the rest home lobby clutching her alligator purse on her lap with both gloved hands. When she was asked what she was doing, she explained she was waiting for her daughter to come fetch her and take her home.

"That wasn't manipulative," I start, but Mother interrupts.

"She knows I can't bring her home to live with us," Mother says.

Yes, you could, I think. You have a huge house; Dad makes plenty of money now; you could hire a nurse. It's not fair. Granny took you in and supported all of us during the war; she lent Dad the down payment for our house in Sausalito. She clerked in a downtown department store for years, on her feet all day; she sewed our clothes, washed our hair, came over to see us on the bus every Sunday with a string bag of fresh fruit and real butter; she baked biscuits for our breakfasts and pies for our dinners. We owe her.

"You take her then," Mother smiles, wicked.

I close my eyes as Mother veers over the dividing strip. I am thinking of the last time I went to the rest home to see Granny alone, carrying Rachel in my arms, and how I couldn't find her—she wasn't reading the Bible in her room; she wasn't knitting in the garden—and how all the shrunken translucent white-haired ghosts in their chairs along the corridor cried out like seabirds and grabbed for Rachel as we passed and how I hurried, walking faster and faster toward the exit, terrified, fleeing death and old age without ever finding my grandmother whom I love more than any other woman in the world.

1968

I call it exile, this housewife's life in Sacramento, and I seem to be having a nervous breakdown, playing Otis Redding's "Dock of the Bay" continuously, weeping night and day for Martin Luther King, Bobby Kennedy, and, to be honest, for myself—a frightened idle lonely woman living in a rented house with two little girls and a husband who never talks. I tell the children to go into the backyard and play so I can be alone to weep and then I get angry because I can't find them—where have the children gone? Have they run away? After screaming at them to get back inside, I storm into the backyard myself. I climb up into the old fig tree and hide there, watching the hot Valley sunset through its leaves. I hate the heat. I hate the sound of traffic. I long for the Pacific Ocean and the fog and the friends I've not yet met who read books and go to foreign films and sing protest songs marching arm in arm across the Golden Gate Bridge. I long to be part of the world but the world seems apart from me. I press my forehead to the rough bark of the tree and repeat the last lines of the Auden poem that has sustained me throughout this long summer: "Life remains a blessing," I whisper. "Although we cannot bless."

When I've repeated the lines often enough to calm down, I back down the trunk, land heavily on the ground, and hustle my wary daughters into the car. I have a plan. We will drive north, find a small mountain town, move into a house in an apple orchard. The girls will each have their own pony and I will work in a diner during the day and write poems all night. As for Dan! Silent Dan who gave me that Auden book with "To Molly, with compassion" penned inside in his tiny mean script—Dan can go ahead and marry that redheaded secretary I am certain he's sleeping with and stay stuck selling insurance in Sacramento forever.

I head for the freeway but somehow the car takes us straight to Macy's, where I charge new curtains for the dining room and manage to hang them before Dan, flushed and tired from a basketball game with his friends after work, comes home. That night, I ask him if he's having an affair with his secretary. He widens his eyes and says Of Course Not Are You Crazy and I wipe my own eyes and say Yes Actually I Am Crazy and by the end of the evening we have decided that as soon as Gretchen starts first grade, I can place Rachel in day care a few mornings a week and go back to school at Sacramento City College. In the meantime, I can enroll in a correspondence course through UC Extension. They don't have any poetry offerings this year but there is a writing class entitled The Short Story, Theory and Practice.

The course is taught by a woman named Cecilia Bartholomew. I never do meet her and it is just as well I never do, as my feeling for her quickly becomes religious. She is stern and scoldy, sets strict exercises, and reminds me, when I thank her for her patience, that her patience is not without limit. I look for the narrow manila envelope with the bright orange return sticker from Berkeley in the mailbox every week, and I pore over her inked comments on my submissions as I sit high in the fig tree. I think about her assignments (illustrate the three types of dramatic conflict in 150 words; portray a character through action in 250 words) as I shop at the market, take the clothes to the laundromat, scrub the oven. While the children nap or watch cartoons, I write. And rewrite. And rewrite again. I have never tried this hard to please anyone but somehow, I know that trying to please Cecilia Bartholomew is going to save my life.

1969

The heater vent runs through the center of the triplex we have moved to in San Francisco and at night I hear everything. The couple upstairs screams at each other and the couple downstairs curses. I am fascinated by their troubles and often slip out of bed to crouch by the vent in my long flannel nightgown, eavesdropping. The fights upstairs have to do with drinking, I discover; the fights downstairs have to do with infidelity. Dan and I never fight. I can't get him to raise his voice or slam a door. I've tried. I sigh as I come back to our bed. I have scarcely closed my eyes before I hear the words: *Kill him.*

I sit up. The words have not come from the vent. The voice is my own and the man I am speaking to stands in the bedroom doorway. He is a stranger to me, tall and stoop-shouldered. It is too dark to see his face. But I can see he holds a gun. *Kill him*, I repeat. I point to the pillow where Dan lies with one bare arm flung over his head and his smooth throat exposed. The stranger approaches, leans over, presses the gun against Dan's heart, and fires.

There is no sound but Dan's chest opens like a flower. His eyes open too. He turns to me. "Honey?" he asks. Blood pools from his parted lips.

I leap out of bed. This has been a dreadful mistake. "We have to get him to the hospital," I chatter. "Hurry! We have to get him over the bridge and to the hospital at once."

The stranger nods, props Dan up, and carries him out to the hall and down the front stairs to a car parked on the street below. Just before they drive away Dan turns to look up at me. His expression is serene and trusting and sweetly loving. There is no blame in it. I collapse to my knees in gratitude. Dan will live. The doctors will save him. No harm has been done. And then I see that the car is not going toward the bridge and the hospital. It is going the other way, toward the country. This stranger is not going to save Dan. He is going to do exactly what I'd asked him to do. He is going to kill him.

I wake up in terror. It is dawn; the house is silent; Dan sleeps beside me. I touch his chest. It is warm and firm and dry and intact. His heart beats innocently beneath my hand. He stirs and turns and reaches for me. I settle back down beside him but I keep my eyes open and as soon as it is light, I slip out of bed and go into the kitchen and cook his favorite breakfast, and then I wake Gretchen and Rachel and we bring French crepes and bacon back to Dan on a tray.

1970

I wish we didn't have to see the parents so often, but now
that we're living in San Francisco, we're stuck. Every Sunday,
over the bridge we go, dutifully driving to visit one set or
the other. My parents in Kentfield are bad enough—the ice
rattling in my mother's highball glass as she talks about the
men she should have married, my father's slippered footsteps
disappearing down the hall—but at least they don't talk poli-
tics. Dan's father in Fairfax is a table pounder. He's still mad
at FDR. He'd still like to bomb Cuba. He hates the Rus-
sians, the Japanese, the *New York Times*, and China. He wants
this Vietnam Thing cleaned up once and for all. If it takes
more troops and planes and Agent Orange—well, that's what
it takes. Wars are made to be won and we're winning—no
thanks, he'll say, to jokers like a certain young couple who go
on peace marches and for what? The fresh air?

Dan doesn't mind these rants as much as I do. He smiles
and rolls his eyes while his father thunders and his mother sits
on the couch cuddling her poodle, whispering love songs into

his greasy black curls, and Gretchen and Rachel and I play dominoes on the coffee table in front of the unlit fireplace.

"Do we have to go?" I ask as usual, watching the city lights trail behind us as once again we head to Marin.

Dan doesn't answer. He knows I know why we have to go. We owe the parents thanks for feeding us, housing us, and lending us money in times of need. Plus, we love them. I lean my forehead against the car window and look up at the moon. Both Dan's parents and mine believe that men actually landed there. I don't. No one knows this, but ever since the first Kennedy was shot, I don't believe a single thing I read in the papers.

1971

Slouched in the doorway, a man watches me. It is too dark to see his face and for a second, I am reminded of my dream about the stoop-shouldered assassin, but then I see, with a tiny secret start, that it is Richard, the husband of my neighbor's sister. I have been thinking about Richard recently. I like his looks, his thick honey-colored hair and the lazy right eye behind his tinted glasses, and I like the way he trembles when he talks to me. I am the only person, his wife says, who can make him laugh at these parties.

When Richard extends his hand, I put down my glass, leave Dan's side, and weave through the crowded room to take it. Richard's fingers are thin and red and cold; they have small dark cuts in them from the stained glass panels he makes in his studio. I have only seen one of his pieces, a cockatoo perched on a grapevine, and despite its rich colors the panel repelled me somehow. Why was his cockatoo so dejected? So sad? Shouldn't it lift its head? Straighten its shoulders? Why did it hunch on its vine like something wounded or ill?

"Where are you two going?" his wife calls.

We pause. His wife has a warm husky voice, always trembling on tears. She is five years older than Richard, has two teenage children, and just had her license suspended for drunk driving. My neighbor has confided that she cheats on Richard, though he doesn't know it, and is currently sleeping with her instructor at the art academy.

"Just getting more wine," Richard answers. He leads me downstairs to a piano in the basement, sits down, and begins to play. It's a song, he says, he wrote for me. It is the saddest song I have ever heard and I have to steady myself against the piano in order not to fall as I listen.

"This song breaks my heart," I say. I look at Richard's downcast eyes, his long fingers on the keys. "You break my heart," I say.

Richard nods but says nothing. There is nothing to say. It is already clear: we are going to break a lot more hearts than our own.

1972

I am going to spend a week alone at a writers' conference in the Sierras. Dan has driven me to the bus depot; he and the girls have blown kisses and waved goodbye. I have left them a freezer full of casseroles, notes under their pillows, promises to return with gifts. I have never gone away alone before, never spent time among real writers before; what can I possibly offer? The story I wrote in my correspondence course for Cecilia Bartholomew was accepted by a magazine, but the magazine went out of business the month my story was to appear, and I have not sold anything else.

I turn away from the window as the bus leaves San Francisco and starts over the Golden Gate Bridge. I try not to stare at the other conference student, a young poet, adjusting his Walkman over his ears. In his torn turtleneck and ponytail, he looks more like a writer than I, in my carefully pressed cotton dress, ever will. But oh! to be a writer! I feel my heart expand with the old longing. To have a book! To be read! I don't want much, just a few perfect pages of a few perfect words; I don't want to be like my mother, who swears she will never write again; I just want to be able to say what I don't yet know how to say in a way that says it so well even I understand it—if that makes sense, which I suspect it does not.

I shake my head and open my bookbag. Is it still there? Yes, among the pens, pencils, notebooks, and my thin sheaf of typed manuscripts, folded tight, tucked deep in a corner, Richard's work phone and address. I should throw it away; it's the last thing I need. Because I need, I need…

I take a deep breath. I need help. I need an awful lot of help.

1973

Dan takes two of the five crystal wine glasses. I keep the other two. We want to throw the fifth glass into the fireplace but the girls and I are renting an old house in Marin now and it has no fireplace, so we throw it into the trash. Dan takes his records and books, but because he has bought a sports car, he leaves me the VW. I need it for my morning job answering phones at the janitors' office and my afternoon job typing insurance forms at the psychiatrists' office and my weekend job cleaning houses in Tiburon and my night classes in the city. The convertible top leaks when it rains and the tires are thin but the radio works fine. I turn it up as I cruise off the bridge exit and onto Doyle Drive, heading for my first fiction workshop at San Francisco State.

Joy of Cooking comes on. I can't believe it—what good luck, my favorite song: "Beginning Tomorrow." I try to belt the lyrics, but my voice is thin from all the nights I've spent drinking red wine, fighting with Dan on the phone, and crying in the bathtub while the girls watch television downstairs, and I waver, several beats behind. The song ends far too soon but if I'm lucky, really lucky, the next song will be "I Can See Clearly Now"—and it is! A sign! This means I am going to get through this time of debt and grief and tears and terror; we won't starve; Dan will start to pay child support on time; Richard will leave his wife, quit the job he hates, record some of his beautiful songs, make a fortune, and marry me; Gretchen will stop pounding *fuckyoumomfuckyoumom* over and over on my typewriter; Rachel will not slip into my bed in the middle of the night saying, "Mommy, I dreamt my left foot was stuck in bad luck"; I will become a good writer at last; all will be well.

It just depends on this next song.

1974

I am driving Gretchen and Rachel back to Marin after retrieving them from Dan's new apartment on Union Street. Dan's twenty-three-year-old girlfriend has French braided the girls' hair and painted their fingernails scarlet, and they are not glad to see me. Gretchen crawls into the back seat and lies face down; Rachel sits in front describing the entire plot of a movie the girlfriend took them to. As always after a weekend with Dan, both girls have picked up his more irritating mannerisms; they widen their eyes like he does and say things like har-de-har.

I've missed them these last two days. I thought I would have time to write, but all I have done is journal endlessly about Richard. He is so depressed! He groans in his sleep! Is it my fault? Am I ruining his life too? The therapist I am seeing at the county hospital gives me a mantra to repeat: *I reject all feelings of blame, shame, guilt, and remorse.* If I did that, I tell him, I'd have no feelings left at all. The therapist frowns. He is barely above five feet tall; his little feet don't touch the floor when he sits; his scuffed white Keds swing back and forth. I am shamefully attracted to him and in order to hide it I chatter on about my two sisters, whom I envy, for both Bridget and Nora are happily married, and about my brother Danny, who has a glamorous life playing keyboards in a rock band. I tell him how my father introduced me to his dentist as "M'daughter, a nice girl but she has no morals," and how my mother phones me almost every morning at six-thirty in tears. My mother's hands are cramped with rheumatoid arthritis; when I visit her, she holds them up and says, "Look what you did to me!" She can no longer paint or play the piano, and as for writing! She never could write! She has never been any good at writing and she is discouraged, she sobs, by the very effort it takes to be mediocre. If only I knew what it is like to be her!

As if, I tell the tiny therapist, I have ever known anything else.

The winter sky over the bay glows green, gold, violet, and apricot as the girls and I join the traffic on the bridge. Gretchen has started to kick the back seat and Rachel has twisted around to slap at her leg and get her to stop it. "Look at the sunset!" I order. I want to get my daughters' attention, to make them like me again, and I take my hand off the steering wheel to point, almost rear-ending the car ahead of us. I brake so hard Rachel flies into the windshield, head first. Panicked, I drive straight to Marin General Hospital, where Rachel is checked for concussion and released. As we're returning to the car she stops to marvel at the spiderweb of glass on the windshield.

"My head did that," she says, awed.

"Look at the sunset," Gretchen says, a phrase both girls repeat to this day.

1975

Mother is in UCSF Hospital again, and my sister Bridget has flown in from New Hampshire to help out. Bridget is efficient, calm, and quick; she does everything well. The only thing she can't do is drive over the bridge. She and her husband live in a rural community and the rush and roar of Bay Area traffic paralyzes her. Alone in Dad's big car, she is helpless. She can't see. She can't breathe. She gets as far as the Marin Headlands before she has to pull over to gasp for air. Forgetting that winters are warm here and that most San Franciscans deplore the wearing of furs, she has thrown Granny's old beaver coat over her jeans; she is flushed and sweating, unable to go forward, unable to turn around and go back. By the time a patrolman finds her, she has almost passed out. He explains that she is having a panic attack, that visitors often have them. He gives her a white paper bag; it smells like fast food and makes her gag, but she takes it and breathes into it, as, lights flashing, the patrolman leads her safely into the city.

She is still upset that night when she tells me about it but I am amused. It's such a good story. I can't resist writing about it. My night class at San Francisco State loves the story and so does the editor I met at Squaw Valley, who accepts it. I am too proud of being published not to brag to my family, even though *Playgirl*, with its nude male centerfold, can only be bought over the counter. The magazine has changed the story's title to "Night Cries," printed it in white type on black paper, and inserted it between ads for something called Sta-Hard Cream. When I give Mother a xeroxed copy (I cannot bring myself to show her the magazine itself), she looks up, confused about the mother character in the story. "Darling," she asks, "who's the bitch?" I hold my breath and chirp, "Diane's mother," which, with a nod, she accepts. But Bridget's not buying it, and when Bridget reads the description of the panicked girl in the beaver coat looking bulky, she stops speaking to me. This is one of the first but far from one of the last trespasses I will make in my writing. You'd think I'd learn, but no, thirty years later I put Bridget into yet another story and again have to beg her forgiveness, which again is withheld, and with very good reason.

1976

"It's not cheating," Dr. K flares. He slaps the Medi-Cal form down by my typewriter. His silver squash blossom necklace bangs against my shoulder and his four huge turquoise rings tap against my desk. Avoiding the silver belt buckle which fronts me, my eyes settle on the fringe of his buckskin jacket. I have never talked back to any of the psychiatrists I work for before. I have heard Dr. J refer to a patient as a cunt and I have seen Dr. D circle his finger around his temple and roll his eyes as he followed another patient out the front door. I have filed Dr. P's letters to his yacht builder asking how many pounds of lead he needs for his ballast trim, and I have put screamers on hold to place telephone orders for the cases of the Châteauneuf-du-Pape Dr. S wants delivered for his dinner parties. The most rebellious thing I've done in the four years I've worked here is change the word "seductive" to "vulnerable" in a court report Dr. T dictated to me describing a five-year-old rape victim. But what am I to do about Chris's Medi-Cal form? Chris jumped off the bridge last month.

How can Dr. K claim he saw him in his office three times since? Isn't that cheating?

"No," Dr. K explains, furious. "If a patient says he's going to kill himself, he's going to kill himself and there's nothing I or anyone else can do about it. I saw Chris four extra times before he jumped, if you'll recall, and I see no reason why I should not be paid for appointments missed since he jumped. And if you think that's cheating, maybe you should"—see a shrink, I finish silently—"look for work elsewhere," Dr. K says.

I would like to, but where would I go? I can walk to this office from home after the girls leave for school and my duties, answering phones, typing insurance forms and court reports, filing the day's mail, and emptying the rain buckets from the leaks in the roof, are easy. Often, bending over the Selectric with the Dictaphone prongs digging into my ears, I can work on one of my own short stories, with none of the doctors being any the wiser. At noon I can take my sandwich, smuggle a few patient files under my sweater, and go up to the conference room to read them. I keep thinking I will learn something from these files, something that will help me be a better writer or even help me understand my own problems, but the narratives I scan are so dark and sad and hopeless that I often return to my desk feeling dirty, shamed, and sickened.

So why don't I stop? Why don't I take Dr. P's professional advice to the catatonic who drools on the waiting room couch and "just snap out of it"?

What is wrong with me?

Paul is usually downstairs when I return to slip the files back in their cabinets. I used to be afraid of Paul, as I am frankly still afraid of most of the schizophrenics who wander in here from the hospital across the street, but Paul has always seemed simple and harmless. Today, however, he is excited, and plucks at my elbow before I can slip past him and into the safety of my cubicle. "I've figured it out," he says. His eyes are luminous. "You see"—and he slaps one dramatic hand to his right shoulder—"my father's blood comes in this side of my body and"—he slaps his other hand to his left shoulder—"my mother's blood comes in this side. And when they meet in my heart"—his eyes gleam—"they fight!"

"Knock it off, Paul," Dr. D says as he comes in to refill his coffee cup. He takes a sip and looks at me. "You don't have to take this, you know. Just tell him to go away. He'll go."

He does. But his words don't. Mother's blood, hot and hurt, on one side, Father's blood, cold and critical, on the other. Unfortunately, though, my parents never fought. They get along great. It's me.

1977

Richard has bought tickets for the symphony tonight and I am looking forward to going. It will be a married date, just the two of us, and the quiet drive into the city will give us time to talk, really talk. The girls will be fine on their own; they will be glad to see us go. They don't like us much these days. We don't like us much either. Richard has been coming home later and later recently, tired from work, too tired to listen to me chat about my job at the psychiatrists' office and my writing classes at State. I follow him as he plods from room to room, dropping his jacket, his spare change, his shoes. What I really want to talk about are his songs—his beautiful songs—because every time he sits down to the piano, which happens less frequently now, I can't help it, I hear money. I want Richard to record his songs and send them to an agent; I want him to quit working for his father in a job he hates; I want him to be famous! He is so talented! He deserves to be famous.

Crossing the bridge on our way to the Civic Auditorium, Richard sighs and pats my hand. I want to hear what he's been thinking about? Fine, he'll tell me. He can run four miles on the treadmill now without stopping; he did fifty leg presses but needs to work on his abs. He's losing his glutes. He has decided to stop dairy, dairy is bad, I should not still be giving it to the girls. It's ruining Gretchen's skin. And as for sugar? Don't get him started on sugar.

Patient, I listen. Patient, I wait. This is not the man I worked so hard to get to marry me. Where is the man I fell in love with, that delicate trembling musical genius? This is not the way the two of us should be living. "Don't you want to do more with your life?" I ask.

But Richard is looking for a place to park where we won't be mugged and doesn't answer. Our seats at the symphony hall are next to a middle-aged gay couple who dress alike, in white linen suits. They hold hands and whisper. During the second movement of the Mahler, I fall asleep against one white shoulder and feel myself being gently—but firmly—pushed upright, back toward my rightful mate.

1978

My creative writing professor has ridden his bicycle across the bridge from his home in San Francisco to visit his friend and my next-door neighbor, but the neighbor is not home so Dr. Litwak sits in my backyard and has a beer with me at the picnic table. It is the first time we have talked outside of class. He is upset about his daughter who is fifteen. She recently brought a strange man home, led him straight past Dr. Litwak with no introduction, took him into her bedroom, and locked the door. They were in there for seven hours.

"What did you do?" I ask.

"I knocked," Dr. Litwak, says, "and asked if they wanted a sandwich."

We laugh. The girl's mother is crazy, Dr. Litwak goes on, and his daughter had a frightening childhood, never knowing whether her mother was going to jump out a window or overdose. He should have sued for child custody when they divorced, but fathers didn't do that in those days and now it's too late. "In any event," he says, his voice breaking, "I did my child a disservice."

I tell him that I too have failed as a parent, that my daughters are also angry and unhappy. We sip our beers in silence. Before Dr. Litwak leaves on his bike he asks me to call him Leo and kisses me on the lips—I am too surprised to turn aside in time although for the next forty years of our deep and abiding friendship, I will always want to. Leo is a terrible kisser, mouth wet and open like a one-year-old's.

1979

Devon, thirty-six hours old, sleeps in the back seat beside me as Richard and I leave Kaiser hospital and all its complications behind and head home. Someday I will tell Devon about my toxemia and how we both could have died, but now all I can think is that we have the rest of our lives to be together. I look down at her exquisite, squinched, rosebud face and smile up at Richard behind the wheel who is still—no—really?—wearing his surgical mask, and then I think of my mother, who phoned this morning to tell me that she too is in a hospital—she'd fallen again and broken her elbow and the pain, she told me, not waiting to hear about Devon, was "excruciating." No matter: Gretchen and Rachel will be waiting on the front porch to welcome their new sister home; our yellow cat Buffy will greet us from the roof and our chocolate lab Almond Joy will race around us in circles. Dad has stopped saying how much he liked Dan and Dan has stopped saying how much he hates me; even Richard's ex-wife sent a nice note and his father has stopped calling Richard Richie.

All this and it's a beautiful day. The world outside our car windows looks newer than it ever has, clouds bright above, bay waters glinting below, everything so fresh and clean—it's as if the world too has just been born.

1980

Richard loves the baby more than me. I complain about this to a friend who calmly says, "Who wouldn't?" Well. It's true I am not loveable these days. Neither is he. The old house we bought in Woodacre takes all our time and we do nothing but quarrel. I spend the days nursing Devon, painting bed-rooms, sanding woodwork, sewing curtains, and digging up weeds in the garden. Rachel helps and so does Gretchen, but we are all overwhelmed. Our house has what the realtor calls "character," but it doesn't have a working furnace or a good septic system, needs doors and floors and a new roof and, most important to me, doesn't have a room where I can write. I type on the dining room table, the dog scratching at the door, Devon calling from her crib. Nothing I write has been any good for months, and although I have published two sto-ries in my lifetime, the rejections are getting me down.

After crumpling another No from the post office in my fist and tossing it into the stone fireplace, I sneak a cigarette from Gretchen's purse and go sit down by the creek to smoke it. Buffy comes and sits beside me and we watch the laurel leaves gather and skeeters scoot across the glossy brown water. I am content until Crazy Brian across the creek bursts into voice. "You can't just go around *bothering* people," he bellows and then he actually emerges through the brush, naked as usual, with a turban of Saran Wrap around his dreads and a bucket in his hands to appease The Water Gods. We've been told not to worry, Brian's delusional but harmless, just another young victim of LSD, but I rise and Buffy and I quickly trot back inside and lock the back door.

Because I have nothing to show to the writing group tonight, I drive to the city with a story I have copied from *The New Yorker*. It's called "The Scent of Lime Trees," and is about a young wife who gives a dinner party for academics and while the men are all cleverly discussing Tolstoy and his estate at Yasnaya Polyana she is on her hands and knees picking grains of spilled rice up from the carpet. "So true," the women in the group and I agree. "So unfair what we have to put up with. So hard to keep it all together."

And yet to say my actual life is hard would be untrue. Yes, Richard is depressed and comes home from work groaning, "Another wasted day," before flopping down on the couch, but he is tender sometimes too, and sometimes still plays the piano. Yes, my mother has had a terrible amputation on her foot and may face another soon, but she tells me I'm her joy and I tell her, truly, meaning it for once, that she's mine. Nora has been in the hospital with undiagnosed internal bleeding and is getting transfusions, but her husband is by her side; Bridget's letters refer to problems she doesn't divulge, but she will be coming to visit soon; Danny's daughter was born with cerebral palsy, but he and his wife are finding comfort in church. Gretchen is in an abusive relationship with the young man we've hired to dig a drainage ditch around the house, but she'll be leaving for college in Long Beach soon, and Dan and Richard have finally agreed to co-fund Rachel in the costly private high school of her choice. I'm slowly losing my pregnancy weight on The Scarsdale Diet, the girls and I still squat, grunting, to *Buns of Steel* and gather together on the couch to watch *The Mary Tyler Moore Show,* and the baby! Devon is so beautiful and inquisitive and bossy and strong—we all love the baby.

I hope the story I have just started will get written someday, and I hope I will be able to share it at next month's writing group and that Lorre won't sigh and say, "I don't know how seriously I am supposed to take this," and Jane won't frown and say, "How can this character be a mother?" Because, oh I still want to be a writer. More than ever. It's just that I'm not writing.

1981

Gretchen comes out of the San Francisco Juvenile Hall still stoned. Driving back to Marin across the bridge, both of us avert our eyes from the crash site: the glass and twisted metal have been swept up from the toll booth but the barrier she hit on Doyle Drive four hours earlier still tips like a tombstone. Thermos full of tequila, purse full of pot, blood count 0.13, defective headlight, 60 mph in a 25-mph zone, car totaled—the second car she's totaled—I glance at her as she slumps, one hand over her mouth where her front teeth once were. Those same front teeth that cost me thousands in orthodontia, that kept me working four jobs, groveling for support payments from Dan, doing my best to placate her dentist—costly teeth, lost now, four white jags on the floor of her towed Olds—how could you, I want to say, do this to me?

Me? What does this have to do with me? I laugh at my own vanity and Gretchen turns, horrified, her wounded mouth black as a vampire's. I reach for her hand. Crossbite, underbite, overbite—for six years this stoic child with the dilated pupils endured stray wires that chewed the inside of her cheeks to raw pink rags. She suffered bands that bit, retainers that scraped the roof of her mouth, headgear that tore and tangled the strands of her fine blonde hair. She never complained. She is not complaining now. "I'm sorry, honey," I say.

She pulls her hand away.

And I want to slap her.

1982

Two o'clock on an April Wednesday and I'm stuck in traffic, late to see Mother who is at UC Hospital once again after yet another amputation. I have been asked to bring her a package of Kents and she will be lying in her private room on the seventh floor, I know, wanting them and getting madder and madder. But what can I do? The commute traffic from Marin has been terrible and now there's an accident on the bridge. The south lanes are stalled, and the north lanes have been closed off. Minutes pass. It's so still I can feel the span sway and hear the raw creak of the wind through the girders. There's a Falcon parked to the left of me, a Mustang behind, and right in front of me, an ambulance, with a woman in curlers and a housecoat propped up on a stretcher. The curtains of the ambulance are open and the woman is staring straight at me. I give a small smile to comfort her, but her pale glazed eyes don't move. My god. Is she dead? She's dead! I'm stuck in traffic behind a dead woman!

"Oh Molly," Mother laughs, wiping her eyes, when I tell her. "What a story!" She lights one of the Kents and leans back on her pillow, exhaling prettily through the red lipstick she put on earlier for the silver-haired priest. Mother has recently converted to Catholicism. She blows smoke at me when I snort. "It's Father L.E.A.C.H., Molly, not L.E.E.C.H.," she says. "Now tell me what else you've been up to."

I can still smell the priest's Eau Sauvage as I chat on, the scent mingled with antiseptics, hospital food, wilted roses, and human blood. I tell Mother about Devon's preschool teacher, who has just been arrested for growing hallucinogenic mushrooms in her basement, about Rachel's wallet, which has been stolen twice from her bookbag at her private high school, about Gretchen's courtship by a forty-year-old Lithuanian who brings deerskin bags of uncut emeralds to the diner where she waitresses, about Richard's depression, the dog's bad back, the cat's kidney disease, the worker who fell through the roof of our house in Woodacre and dangled there, legs swinging over the piano until one of his crew pulled him out, about my overcrowded classes at State, and the rejection I just got from *Redbook* magazine, saying that the profession of my story's protagonist wasn't "careaboutable" but if I could rewrite and make her a book reviewer instead of a poet, they would be glad to reconsider publishing me.

Mother listens, smoking, flexing her new stump under the sheet. "I'm just so glad," she finally says, as she stubs her cigarette out in the ashtray she hides in the bed stand, "that I'm not you, darling." She lifts a hand to my father, just stepping through the door. "At last," she calls. "I thought you'd never get here. Did you bring the G.I.N.?"

1983

Mother wants to come to my Short Story Writing class. She and her friend Betty have been taking an emeritus class at College of Marin but they don't like the teacher and they don't feel they are learning anything. It would be a big help to both of them, Mother says, to sit in on a class of younger students. Getting to San Francisco State over the bridge of course is a problem now that she can't drive, but luckily Betty's hip is better since her surgery and she knows how to fold the wheelchair into the trunk of her car just fine, plus she can use Mother's disabled sticker so parking in the city won't be a problem. The Humanities Building *does* have an elevator, does it not? And a women's lavatory? Is there a cafeteria nearby? Mother will be fine once they get to my classroom on the second floor and Betty can wheel her right in. So what time is the class? Betty thinks it's from noon to one but Mother clearly remembers seeing noon to two-thirty on the schedule.

"There are thirty-five students in my classroom already, Mom. I can't take any more. I don't have room for you."

But she will only be *auditing*, Mother explains. She won't be signing up or anything. Neither will Betty. In fact, Betty may not even participate; she may just stand in the back and Mother herself won't take up any room; she likes to sit in front anyway, where she can hear—"You're not still mumbling, are you?" she stops to ask me. "You *are* speaking up? You were such a mumbler as a child, what did we used to call you, oh yes, 'Missy Mushmouth'"—so she'll probably just wheel in close to my desk, maybe sit just to one side of my desk in front. Will that make me uncomfortable?

"Yes."

Well, it shouldn't.

"Mom, you can't audit my class."

But I won't even know she's there! She will wear her dark glasses and put her mink coat over her *prosthesis* and be quiet as a little mouse. I won't have to introduce her; no one needs to know that she's my mother or that she herself published a novel in 1947 that was a bestseller in the Bay Area and got reviewed in the *New York Times*. She won't talk about herself. She just wants to get back into writing! What could be simpler? She has a million questions about literature and a few, frankly quite a few, good ideas for topics. All she needs is to confirm the time, oh, and my room number. She wrote it down but she lost it. Could I tell her again?

"No."

Just a second while she looks for a pencil. One more time?

"No."

And don't worry about cigarettes. She can go without smoking for a few hours; she's done it before, unless it's permitted somewhere in the building…?

"No."

Well, not to worry. She'll be fine. And Betty doesn't smoke at all!

1984

The huge bouquet of helium balloons is delivered midafternoon to the fiction workshop I am teaching and although my students clap, I am horrified. Winning the Flannery O'Connor Award for my story collection is something I savor in secret; I almost don't want anyone to know about it. This public acknowledgment, a gift from an older colleague, demands that I rise to the occasion, that I celebrate myself, and I can't. I'm not good enough. Flannery O'Connor has been my hero for years; to be in her shadow is an honor and a humiliation, both—I don't belong; I should not intrude. I blush and read the accompanying card out loud to my class but I am not happy. I try to explain: I based the collection on my thesis, I tell them, and if they continue to work on their own theses, they may win an award themselves someday. I submitted to the O'Connor three times, I continue: the first time I got a note back from the editor saying that I had been a finalist but that the judges ultimately had not liked several of the stories. The next year I submitted again, deleting and replacing the offending stories (which were, of course, my best, I lie) and again the editor wrote back to say I had been a finalist but the judges were still unenthusiastic about some of the stories. The third time I submitted—and "submitted," I tell my students, is the verb writers try not to choke on—I fine-tuned the collection and I won!

"So, you had a lot of faith in yourself," one of the students says.

"Not at all! I'm just stubborn."

"False humility," another student says.

I shake my head, unable to explain, even to myself, how this success has both thrilled and mortified me. I tie the huge bobbing balloons to the back of a chair until workshop is over. Back in the mail room, the bouquet bouncing off my wrist, I find yet another note from the older colleague in my box; a love poem. I do not understand his poems and I have told him I do not want to receive them. I am friends with his wife; he is friends with Richard; I want this to stop. I have asked Richard to talk to him but Richard has only advised me to "be kind." I don't feel kind. I write a quick cold thank you for the balloons and stick it, with the poem which I've torn up, in his mail slot.

Driving home over the bridge, the balloons bat wildly back and forth in the back seat, blocking the windows so I can scarcely see out and irritating me even more. How to get rid of them? I could pull over at Vista Point and release them over the Bay. Or hey! My brother Danny's wife just had a baby! I swing by Marin General Hospital where Bonnie is recuperating in bed and hand her the bouquet. Bonnie looks up from the Bible she's been reading and blinks; she clearly doesn't want this gift any more than I do. "Pass them on," I say gaily. "Someone must like balloons!"

1985

Mom is dying on the same day my book is to be launched. "Go to the party," Mom insists. "I'll be fine. Hospice is here, and Bridget and Nora can handle everything." I hesitate. Mom, who has said nothing about my stories except to wonder why they "are all so sad," has sent copies of my book to everyone in the family with a single note inside: *I have a terminal illness.*

"Go," she urges. "I want you to go."

I want to go too but for the first time in my life I understand what it means to feel "torn"—I literally feel a zigzag rip down my middle. I turn to Dad. He doesn't look up from the newspaper he is reading, just lifts one hand and waves bye-bye. Bridget is already baking wheat bread in the kitchen and Nora is talking to the nurse. Telling myself this launch is not for me, it's for my book, the book I have been cuddling close to my heart like a baby, I put on the cerise-colored sheath I bought to match the inner flap of my beautiful book, leave Devon with a sitter, and take off for the city with my friend Judy.

Judy drives. Richard is working late but has said he will meet us at the bookstore. As we head over the bridge Judy asks, "Has Richard even read your book?"

"He's never read anything I've written."

"Like Dan," Judy points out.

Minerva's Owl is already crowded when we arrive and I am given a glass of wine and hustled off to a table for signing; friends and colleagues crowd around. A half hour passes and then another. People start to leave, and no sign of Richard until at last he slips in, smiling, had to work late, couldn't find a parking place, lotta traffic out there. We are silent on the drive back home and when I start to cry on the bridge, he thinks it's only for my mother.

She is still alive when we get back, and she lasts until Sunday morning. Bridget and Nora and I sit around her bed, taking turns holding her hand; Danny, uneasy, stands half in and half out of the doorway; Dad comes in from time to time to peer down at her pale face and hold a mirror to her lips; the poodle pads around, confused and overfed. At one point Mom opens her eyes, which have turned a milky turquoise, raises her head up, and announces, "I am so frustrated," before falling back upon the pillow. My sisters and I look at each other. We do not want our fierce and beautiful mother to die like this, feeling that her life has been a failure. We tell her how much we love her; how proud of her we are. When her breath changes into the brain stem rhythms the hospice nurse has taught us to recognize, we crowd even closer. "She's going," I say at last. "Going," Bridget echoes. "Gone," Nora intones. And the last thing our mother hears, if she hears anything at all, and we pray she does not, is the sound of her three daughters laughing.

1986

A young writer I met at a summer workshop has invited me to meet her for lunch on Sacramento Street. I arrive early, park, and window-shop as I make my way toward the restaurant. This is what I think of as a fancy neighborhood, lined with expensive stores; I pass displays of antiques and jewelry and designer dresses and pause before an entire shop full of nothing but cloaks. Cloaks! Cream-colored cashmere cloaks lined in plum and peach and royal blue! Where would you wear such a cloak and who would be regal enough to carry one off?

At lunch over our salads, the young writer asks if I would be willing to teach a private class at her home once a week. She is working on a story about her family and she hasn't been getting much help from the writers group she's in; it's composed mainly of men—she calls them boys—who write about binge drinking and baseball. She proposes a small class with just her and a few other friends, all women. They are willing to pay.

I hesitate. Because I am teaching part-time both at San Francisco State and the University of San Francisco, I don't need extra money right now—but if I divorce Richard, as I long to do, I will need quite a bit of extra money, and soon. I thank the young writer and say I will think about it, but what I am thinking about as I return across the bridge is not the class nor my troubles with Richard nor my attraction to the bearded carpenter who has recently come to work on our house, but the cloaks. My mother could have gotten away with wearing one of those cloaks. I can see her now, flipping one scarlet edge over one white shoulder. She would have looked gorgeous. Why did I never give my mother a cloak? I should have!

"Mama," I cry. I have never called my mother Mama before in my life. She would have hated it. She made Rachel and Gretchen and Devon call her Grandmere. "Mama," I cry, alone in my car, "Mama, oh Mama!"

1987

I know my stepmother's hand; it has been raised to me in anger often enough, and I recognize those thick digits with their fake red nails splayed on the steering wheel of the Mercedes cruising in the bridge lane beside my car. Her sprayed blonde pouf, her hawk-nosed profile, yes, it's my father's new wife all right, the woman he married a few months after Mom died, the handsome socialite who condemns me for leaving Richard and taking up with the carpenter, who forbids me to see Dad, who will not let me inside her home unless, and I quote, "Molly crawls in through the back door on her hands and knees," and there, sitting tall in the passenger seat beside her, my nephew, Bridget's son, the Annapolis grad in his white dress uniform. No one told me Benjy was in town. There must have been gala family dinners all week, celebrations I've been excluded from. Why didn't anyone tell me? No, I didn't want Dad to remarry so soon; yes, I wanted him to wait until a year had passed, but I behaved, didn't I, more or less? I actually liked this stepmother when I first met her; I liked that she got Dad to limit his drinking, took him out for walks, and shrugged off his sarcasm. So what if she funded luncheons for Ronald Reagan. So what if she was anti birth control, pro capital punishment, and confused Gore Vidal with Vidal Sassoon. Maybe I rolled my eyes a little too obviously at the engagement party. Maybe I drank too much at the wedding. Maybe I pointed out that fifteen years was a big age difference, maybe I wondered if she knew about Dad's emphysema. But didn't I back down when Dad curtly reminded me his life was none of my business? Didn't I shut up? Didn't I try? My sisters tried harder, that's true. Bridget, just glad "Dad is going to be taken care of," has been nothing but sweetness and light, Nora, fearful of offending, has been silent. Danny, no longer playing in rock bands, couldn't be happier; a licensed stockbroker in Dad's office, Danny is now handling her money.

I hate them all.

I see my stepmother and Benjy chatting, smiling; they do not see me. Oh how I long to veer sideways, fast, and smash that glossy Mercedes through the guardrail and over the edge! Just one swift twist of the wheel and oops so sorry goodbye go to hell.

1988

The carpentry tools and fishing poles rattle in the back of the van as Ken and I head down to Monterey. We are taking Devon and her friend Mariposa to the aquarium and the girls are giggling as they dress and undress their Barbies on the built-in bench behind us. Mariposa's Barbie suddenly pops over the back of the seat and kisses Ken's beard and Ken, startled, slaps at it. "I'm not used to such a fluffy load," he apologizes. He smiles at me. I smile back. Ken is the best-looking man I have ever seen. I know that is no reason to be with someone and I despise myself for being so shallow, but I can't help it: Ken is tall and broad-shouldered and slim-hipped and blue-eyed and curly-haired and his calloused hands are smudged with paint and plaster and his cotton shirts smell like the sun and wind from drying on the clothesline. When he goes to lunch strange women slip their phone numbers onto his table. Does he call them back? I can't tell! I know so little about the life he leads when we aren't together!

"Are you two going to get married?" Mariposa asks, leaning her Barbie forward again. Devon, horrified, tries to pull her back. "Are you?" Mariposa persists.

I open my mouth to say—what can I say? Not yet? Maybe when the divorce from Richard ever comes through? Maybe when Ken starts his own contracting company and I publish another book and finally get tenure? But Ken only laughs. "Who would have us?" he asks, and I settle back, silent, well warned, Devon's relieved sigh in my ear.

1989

Earthquake! From the University of San Francisco campus high on Lone Mountain, I brush off the mosquitoes that have suddenly started to swarm and look down at the city burning below. Sirens shriek and helicopters whir from neighborhood to neighborhood as the orange sunset fades and the city darkens. The Bay Bridge collapsed, the students and I are told; it broke in two, spilling some cars into the ocean below and trapping others in concrete and steel, but the Golden Gate—my strong resilient Golden Gate—will reopen later tonight. All the phone lines are down and I can't reach Devon, who is home alone, scared, I'm sure, but hopefully safe; they are saying West Marin is safe, no damages, so I pace and wait, watching the news on a Beta television set up in the well-lit cafeteria. One of the priests offers hot coffee and I take it, grateful. You Jesuits sure know how to do things, I want to say. But my teeth are chattering too much to talk and anyway, I tell myself, it would take more than working generators to get me to convert.

It is not until two in the morning before I am able to join the long parade of cars heading home across the span. I can barely breathe the entire mile and a half it takes to cross the bridge and it seems to me the drivers to my right and the drivers to my left are holding their breath too. Once across we all hit our accelerators and surge forward, trying to out-race an abyss that could open any second beneath us.

1990

"Who are you doing this for?"

The ski instructor's voice is kind, and for the first time all morning she extends a hand to help me up. I brush my parka off, thank her, and limp back to the lodge to wait for Ken's return from the slopes. Slumping onto an empty bench, I try to tell myself it doesn't matter: I don't have to be a good skier. I tried not to hate the cold and the wet and the four-year-old twins who sped past me effortlessly after two minutes of instruction. It hurts to keep falling, though; it hurts to keep failing.

I rub my bruised hip and stare out the window, thinking about my future. I have to be practical. What if my bid for tenure is again denied, what if my new story collection never gets accepted, what if my divorce from Richard never goes through? The house is in foreclosure because of his debts; can I save it? How? I write at least three book reviews a month but they pay very little. I love my adjunct work at State and USF, and the private classes I teach remain deeply satisfying; the generous energy of the students I work with both exhausts and sustains me, but there is no real money in part-time teaching. I am worried about Devon, eleven years old, lonely, growing so fast. I should never have left her with a sitter this weekend; she needs me. I am worried about Gretchen, miserably married to the old man who offered her emeralds but has provided nothing but coal dust, and about Rachel, trekking through Nepal and "hostessing," whatever that means, in a Tokyo bar after her year working in the bio-chem lab in Israel. I am worried about my dying father, with whom I've never been able to make friends. I am worried about Richard, who is bankrupt and living in a warehouse, and I am worried about Ken, but that's nothing new. There's no future with Ken.

Ken enters the lodge, rosy and brisk, sequins of frost in his beard. He asks how I did with the lesson and laughs when I tell him. We drive back to our campground at the hot springs, where we soak first in a warm pool, then swim in a cool one, then return to the warm one. It is heaven to stretch out in the water and look up while the sunset paints the white winter sky in swaths of peach and lavender. The air, as we trudge back across the snowfield to the van, is odorless, not even the stands of Christmas trees smell Christmas-y here, everything so cold and pure.

We have supper in the van—Ken humming, bent over a pot of chili on the camp stove, me reading by candlelight. I am full of the book I brought with me, Vikram Seth's *The Golden Gate*, which I will be teaching to my graduate class on Tuesday. Without asking if it's all right, I start to read some of the sonnets out loud as we eat.

Ken may be listening or not; I never can tell; it doesn't matter. I look around at the warm candlelit clutter surrounding us and wish there were some way—of course there is no way—of banding it all tight around with a ribbon of gold and keeping it forever.

1991

He doesn't want to see me. I don't care. He's dying and he's my dad and I want to see him and I'm going to the hospital anyway. It's ridiculous that he lets my stepmother keep us apart. "She punishes me when you visit," he explained, his voice low. How? Does she beat him? Does she starve him? Is my dad truly so weak that he lets this crazy woman boss him around? Is he not the hero of my life?

I don't know what to do. I write him a letter every morning and tear it up every afternoon. I say I am sorry we are estranged and then I say he should be sorry and then I say we deserve each other but mainly I say Don't die.

I will not say any of that today. I will sit by his hospital bed and simply give him the news: Gretchen has left the old man at last; she is still waitressing but she has started to write articles for a weekly newspaper; her two little boys are fine. Rachel is back from her travels and doing graduate work at Berkeley; Devon is twelve and stole the show as Fagin in her school's production of *Oliver!* Richard is…well, no one knows how Richard is, or even where he is, there have been sightings of him talking to Iranian salesmen at various rug shops in Berkeley but that's all. I will not mention the foreclosure I am fighting. I will not mention Ken. When I introduced them two years ago, Dad ignored Ken's outstretched hand. "Heard a lot about you," Dad said. "Haven't liked what I've heard," and Ken, surprised into some genius instinct I didn't know he had, laughed. I will not remind Dad of that.

I will tell him about how I won the National Book Critics Circle Award for Book Reviewing last month and was flown to New York and seated next to John Updike at the awards ceremony. I will tell him how I managed to make John Updike laugh and how the hotel was overrun with flocks of merry red-haired children flown in from Ireland to march in the St. Patrick's Day parade. Dad likes hearing things like that.

He does not want to hear about how sad and sorry I am that he and I have failed at being friends. And why would we want to be friends anyway? Dad did what he had to do raising me. He fed me and clothed me. He took me to horseback riding lessons. He zipped my wedding dress up when I married Dan, and although he said, as he did it—too late! too late!—"You don't have to go through with this, you know," he still lent us his Porsche to use on the drive back from Reno. He paid for my year at Berkeley and after I married Dan he continued to send checks—made out to my maiden name, it's true—but checks we needed and probably never properly thanked him for. He was kind to Richard. He found my car keys when they were wedged under Devon's car seat. He may never have said I love you, but he did say Ditto when

I said I loved him, and I always knew he would be there to help me out of trouble.

If I'm lucky today, Dad will let me touch his hand, splotched and bruised, lying on top of the covers with an IV running into it, but I won't expect him to bless me. He won't have to. I already feel blessed, right now, speeding toward him, just knowing that, today at least, he is still alive.

1992

The Russian has a truck bed full of flowering shrubs and a little yellow dog with three legs that sits on my lap during the long ride back to Woodacre. The Russian will not take money or let me pay for the gas. He is too excited. This is a lucky thing, to meet an actual writer stranded by her broken Honda at midnight in the middle of Golden Gate Park, but then, he says, he has always had luck. He was born in Iran and grew up in Morocco and lived in Afghanistan before he came to San Francisco. He is a musician and a juggler. He speaks Russian, Spanish, French, and Farsi. His first unpublished novel was in Farsi; this new one, however, is in English. It is a wonderful novel. His friends love it. But he can't get it published. Hey! the Russian says. Why don't you read it? You are an editor. It is only 746 pages long. It is all about chess. You could help with the grammar—what do you think?

I stroke the little dog's head on my lap and look at the Russian's large hands as they flex on the steering wheel. I would rather be strangled, I think; I would rather be robbed and dumped on the side of the road. But: Yes, I say. Of course.

So then! Here is your house! Here is my manuscript! Can you read my handwriting? *Dasvidaniya*! We'll be in touch.

1993

The office above the Old Western Saloon in Point Reyes Station is small and funky and smells like wood rot and tobacco smoke and even at one-hundred-ten dollars a month is more than I can afford, but I love it. The door locks and there is no telephone. A wooden door balanced on two sawhorses serves as my desk. I have a Xerox computer and a Diablo printer that is so loud that the sand plovers nesting on the gravel roof of Cheda's Garage next door take flight whenever I use it. Every spring the garage owner hires four goats to graze the vacant lot below and I watch them chew their way through the blackberry brambles and weeds until the lot is scraped bare. Day after day, Patsy Cline's "Crazy" wafts up from the jukebox downstairs, and the rhythms of the song shape my sentences as I work on my novel. Sometimes I sing along. Sometimes I lie down on the bare floor and nap. Sometimes I walk up the block to the Bovine Bakery for a hot coffee and a chocolate chip cookie which I eat slowly, gazing into the windows of the dime store and the yarn shop as I walk back.

I rarely stop to say hello to Gretchen, who has moved back to Marin with my grandsons and taken a job waitressing at the Station House Café across the street. "Of all the gin joints in the world," I drawl, and Gretchen shrugs, So what. She won't bother me, she says. But she will. I am bothered just knowing she is there, working hard while I am doing nothing to help her. These brief weeks between semesters are the only times I have to work on *Iron Shoes*, and I don't want to be a good mother or good grandmother during this time. I just don't don't don't. I should probably be home cooking for her boys right now while *she* writes a novel. She's talented. She could write about me, as I, surprise, am writing about my own mother, trying, and so far, it feels, failing, to capture her self-destructiveness, her courage, her anger, and her glamor. I have made Mom far worse on the page than she ever was in real life and I have made the character based on me far nicer.

I shift in my chair, try to steady my desk, type a line, x it out, type another, and stare at the walls.

I have hung two posters on the walls. One is a glossy gray and white photo of John Lennon. I greet him every time I walk in. "Hi, honey," I chirp. "Don't call me honey," John says back. The other poster is one Rachel found in a used bookstore in Berkeley and gave me; it's a cartoon of the Golden Gate Bridge with an enormous pelican and an even larger whale sailing above it. This poster reminds me to take chances with *Iron Shoes*. To get my plot off the ground I have to set it aloft, be more playful with my language, stick in a whale or two. Sometimes when I'm driving over the bridge to my teaching jobs, I look up. Usually, the fog has rolled in and I can't see a thing. Which doesn't mean no whale is up there. Just that I cannot see it. Yet. I will have to work harder.

Leaving my office late one Sunday afternoon, after, again, not working well, I get in my car, try to start it, and realize the battery's dead. I've left the lights on. I've done this three times since I broke up with Ken and I've maxed out my AAA card. I get out, slam the door, take a deep breath, and slowly cross the street to the Café. Gretchen bites back a smirk, unties her apron, gets the cables out of her Volvo and jump-starts my Honda. We don't say much as we stand outside in the foggy dark. She whistles; I hum. It takes me a while to realize we're both humming the same tune: "Crazy."

1994

Devon cries quietly all the way to the airport. She does not want to move to Honolulu. We are not moving, I repeat; it's not permanent, I'm only a visiting writer and I will only be teaching one term at the University in Manoa. We will only stay five months, then leave. It's a great opportunity for me; I won't have to teach so many classes; I can work on my novel; it will give us more money; she should be glad. She'll be back in our old house in Woodacre with her old friends at her old high school in January.

"You'll learn to surf," Ken booms, but we both ignore him. Devon never answers anything Ken says, and I have begun to stonewall him as well. "Don't you want to learn to hula?" he persists, his voice too loud for the car.

Devon shudders and wipes her tears. She is fifteen and a champion crier. Her lovely face never gets red or blotchy; her nose never runs; weeping, she manages to look like an orchid drenched in dew. She has asked me several times why Ken has to come with us to Hawaii and I haven't come up with a good answer. After all, Ken and I don't live together; it's not as if he'll replace Richard or ever be Devon's stepfather. But if he doesn't come with us, won't I lose him again, this time forever?

Ken's nineteen-year-old son is driving us to the airport and he has not yet said a word. Now as he pays the toll with the three dollars I hand him, he snorts and turns to Devon. "Dad will be the one down at the beach taking Hula lessons," he assures her, and Devon sniffles, prettily, and cheers up.

1995

Devon cries all the way coming back from the airport. She is going to miss Adriene and Serena and the handsome water polo player she had a crush on at Iolani. She never wanted to leave Honolulu. She had the best time of her life in Hawaii and now I am forcing her to return to the old house and the old school and the old set of friends who have surely forgotten her by now. She wishes Ken was with us because Ken at least wouldn't laugh at her like I am laughing. Ken wouldn't remind her how she felt last year. Ken would understand.

1996

I have broken off with Ken again, this time for good. My friends are relieved but I feel bleak. *Iron Shoes* still isn't finished and *Creek Walk and Other Stories* hasn't been published. I am teaching four classes a semester, reading scores of graduate applications, and I have seventeen theses to supervise this spring. I'm being stalked by a disfigured parolee who was born with no lips and who stands outside my office in the Humanities Building telling passing students that he would hate to see me "brutalized." A trembling undergraduate comes up as I stand by the blackboard to confide he is carrying a loaded gun in his backpack and is afraid he might use it. An older woman screams that I have totally misread her story and should not be allowed to teach. A colleague has just published a bestselling novel about a divorced woman who supports herself writing book reviews. Gretchen is seeing a new man she met in a bar; she knows I'll like him because he's read *Under the Volcano* four times and when I tell her that even reading that book once gave me a contact hangover she says, "Fine! I guess nothing I do is ever going to please you," and slams out the door. Rachel has moved to the Netherlands with her boyfriend and is never coming back. Devon is about to leave for college in San Diego and says she will come back, but she won't.

Driving to a museum opening, I blab all this and my painter friend Sherry comforts me. Sherry sees beauty in everything. The bridge approach is especially spectacular tonight, she says. There is a pink sunset and the fog tumbling down the Waldo Grade is also tinged pink and look how the tunnel opens its perfect arch to showcase the perfect arches of the bridge. She continues to marvel out loud as we park near the de Young. Walking slowly, for Sherry limps and uses a cane, we cross the Music Concourse in a low mauve mist, the amputated boughs of the plane trees dark above us. The museum needs repair. The nose of one stone Sphinx at the entrance has been broken off but the paws look large and safe and I confess to Sherry that I have always wanted to crawl in and sit between them. She gives me a curious look and asks if I'd like to go to Egypt with a group of women professors she knows. No, I don't want to do anything with a group of women and especially not professors.

Inside the museum I gulp two glasses of white wine and wander through the crowd pretending I am not looking for someone to love me. It can't be any of the men I already know, the friends I meet for walks and lunches and movies, not Roger nor Bill nor Peter nor Tom. They don't want me and the only man I want is a tall rumpled Australian I glimpsed for five seconds at Heathrow years ago; he struck me as bright, articulate, funny, and kind. He reminded me of me, the me I ought to be. I want a man like the me I ought to be.

Driving home, Sherry asks why I ended things with Ken. Was it money? Well yes, I answer, partly, for Ken was as bad as Richard with money, always investing in crackpot schemes, always deep in debt. Was it sex? Not really, but Ken had leg cramps, back cramps, shoulder aches, fibrillation, toothaches, stomach problems, frequent bouts of impotence; he didn't think I was compassionate enough about his physical problems and he was right, I wasn't. Was it because he couldn't commit to a relationship? Well again yes, but only partly. Because: what if he had committed? Then what would I do? I think about the messes he made, sawdust and sand and keys and can openers and loose change and Get Rich Quick pamphlets and Hari Krishna handouts and apple cores and fast-food wrappers and tubes of grout and other women's phone numbers falling out of his pockets with every step he took. "He never made the bed," I say at last. "It was always rumpled. Lumpy. Sheets dragging on the floor. Comforter bunched in a corner."

Sherry nods. "I can see all that." Then she sighs. "But he sure is cute."

1997

Creek Walk and Other Stories has been published after all! And it's getting positive reviews, it's been a bestseller in the Bay Area for the last two weeks and it's listed in the *New York Times* as one of the 100 best books of the year. I'm featured in local newspapers and on radio shows. I have an expensive black Anne Klein suit to wear to the readings I give. My talks are well-attended and my speech at the Kidney Foundation Luncheon is a hit; I sell almost as many books there as Sue Grafton does. I'm promoted to full tenured professor at State. I'm editing a literary magazine. Devon and I go to England for Easter week and Rachel and her partner Scott take the train down from Amsterdam to join us. The cats are alive. The car works. I'm on sabbatical all fall. I will house-sit a friend's penthouse in Honolulu in December and am up to Chapter 19 of *Iron Shoes*. I am happy. I am free.

I am so happy and so free that I invite Ken to dinner one night when I get home from Hawaii. We exchange Christmas gifts; I give him cookies and he gives me a calendar with photos of the Golden Gate Bridge. We do not sleep together but his sweet merry "I'll be seein' you," as he hugs me goodbye at the door rings in my ear for the rest of the night.

1998

The medium is late and the twelve of us, sitting around the dining room table, are awkward and jokey with each other, waiting for the séance to start. We are all writers. Aside from the hostess, I know no one. I have read the novel about the geisha and the memoir about Jonestown, but I will never read the book on the Chinese revolution, and I have not kept up with the novels the pretty South American novelist turns out every year. The woman who wrote about her biological mother sits holding hands with her girlfriend, and the homeless man who wrote about dumpster diving shifts in his seat, laughs to himself, and reaches for another cookie.

When she finally arrives, breathless, her red jacket rumpled, her blonde hair a tangle, the medium, whose name is Sharon, explains that she's late because the spirits crowded into her car the minute she left home and shouted so clamorously she almost crashed twice. "They're at their worst behavior on the bridge," Sharon complains, sitting down at the table. "They don't shut up. Well. Let's start."

She unpacks a microphone and a tape recorder. We may notice lights flickering, she warns us; the centerpiece may tremble. If any of us brought photographs a blue haze may start to hover around them. I glance at the photograph the poet to my right has propped up—a black-and-white print of a dark-haired woman in a fur jacket—and at the gold pocket watch the cookbook writer to my left has placed by her teacup. I have brought nothing. I expect nothing. I am superstitious but I don't believe in ghosts. There are things on my mind—*Iron Shoes* has just been accepted, to my deep relief, amazement, and joy, but it needs so many revisions! Will I be able to make them? Will I have time? I've just been offered a new teaching job. Should I take it? It pays twice what I make at San Francisco State and requires only half the work, and, as an extra added enticement, offers me a six-week summer teaching stint in Ireland, the country I have always longed to visit—but the university itself is in far-off Fayetteville, Arkansas. Should I go? Would Ken come with me if I went? Do I want him to? Are any of these questions the dead can answer?

"No," Sharon says. "They can't predict the future. They can't help that way. The spirits are here—right now, all around us—either because they want forgiveness for something they did or they want help with something that still bothers them. Mostly they want to let us know we are loved. They may announce their arrival with a physical sensation," she continues. "You might feel what they felt the moment they died; a catch in the heart, a dizziness, a sudden stabbing pain."

She smiles around the room, tired, then closes her eyes and begins talking. She calls out name after name and the writers around me cry out in surprised recognition. "Carlos? Does anyone know a Carlos?" I bite back a smile as the mother of the Chilean novelist gasps. I duck my head to hide another smile as Sharon says she sees windmills over the head of another novelist, whose upcoming trip to the Netherlands has been in the society pages. Spirit after spirit checks in to see if their dog has been walked, their library book returned, their letter found. What a crock, I think. Just then, Sharon stops, opens her eyes, and looks straight at me. Her face is pale, her lipstick smudged. "There is a tall man in glasses standing right behind you," she says.

"No way," I protest, "my dad wouldn't be caught dead at a séance."

No one laughs and Sharon, concentrating, shakes her head. "He's gone now," she says.

I'm sure he is, I think. I stop listening and begin wondering how much tip I should leave when suddenly, for no reason, I can't breathe. My eyes burn, my throat fills with a bitter chemical taste, I start to cough. The cookbook writer next to me coughs too and the poet to my right, also coughing, pushes back her chair, stands, and holds up her photograph. "Aunt Emma," she whispers, her voice ragged. "Aunt Emma was gassed at Auschwitz. Aunt Emma was here," the poet asks Sharon. "Wasn't she?"

Sharon, exhausted, nods. The cookbook writer and I look at each other, silent.

When I drive home over the bridge, a half hour later, I almost wish my car could fill, like Sharon's, with voices. How great it would be to hear the dead: my mother's cackle, my grandmother's gentle scold, my best friend's snide little laugh. But I hear nothing, see nothing. All I can think about is that tall man in glasses, my smart, shy, and unamused father, whom I have once again disappointed, this time perhaps forever.

1999

October Sunday in Fayetteville. I awaken to the sound of church bells, train whistles, cardinal calls, rap music from the student who lives below, and heavy footsteps from the stand-up comic who lives above me. The comic leaves notes on my windshield asking if I'd like to meet for coffee. I am terri-fied of him—he's an ex-Baptist minister! he wears overalls! his name is Gomer!—and I haven't answered. If Ken were here...but Ken is not here and it is clear, at this point, he is never going to be here.

I punch the pillow and sit up without disturbing the two old cats I brought with me from California who stay curled on the quilt. I am renting the middle flat of a white triplex with a wide front porch that was built in 1884; the ceilings are high, the floor is hardwood, the bedroom dresser was hand-built by my landlord's grandfather. I make coffee—I am almost out of the Peet's I brought from California—and eat the Arkansas Black apple I bought yesterday at the Farm-ers' Market on the town square. I empty my briefcase onto the kitchen table and sit down to correct student papers; I have asked my undergraduates to write about The Most Important Thing That Ever Happened to Them and nine out of a class of fifteen have written about being born again. Just as I did back in San Francisco, when two of my students wrote about having sex with corpses, I scrawl "Show, don't tell" in the margins and demand rewrites.

The day stretches ahead. Should I walk to the park? The park is green and grassy and lined with tall trees turning amber and russet, but the sidewalks around it are broken bits of bisque, cracked and stained, and there are copperheads in the creek bed below. Should I go to the gym? The last time I went to the gym I saw a colleague from the Creative Writing Department and his wife steadily pumping away on exercise bikes, both reading Chekhov. I had to hide my *Vanity Fair* behind my back. Should I play the piano—I brought my baby grand all the way from California, after all—or watch television on my new 27-inch Sony? Should I go to Walmart? The last time I shopped at Walmart I heard one man in a feed cap greet another with, "Y'all oughta come up to our place. Got a freezer full of squirrel." Should I do what I said I was going to do when I moved here, what I told everyone I was going to do, and start writing a new novel before *Iron Shoes* comes out next year?

Or should I do what I usually do on Sundays, and get in the car and drive? Hoping Gomer won't spot me, I lock the front door and slip into my car. I circle the university first, slowing past the Georgian fraternity and sorority houses, past the wide green lawns and handsome brick administration buildings, then up the hill to the drearier beige blocks where my own classes are held. I am, I've been told, the first "full-time woman" who has ever been hired to teach in my department, which has made me wonder what "part-time women" do in academia around here—desex themselves the minute they come home? Toss their female parts onto the bed as they change into their workout clothes?

I grimace, head down the hill to stop for a frozen custard, thirty-thousand calories of pure Southern bliss, slow to see if the protesters are still camped outside the abortion doctor's office, then drive out of town, past farmlands and strip malls. I see horses and bison herds and heavyset people sitting on their porches playing guitars; I see rivers quietly reflecting limestone cliffs and abandoned barns and smoke coming out of hidden hollows. Once or twice, I've made a wrong turn and ended up in Missouri; once I got lost in a dark pine forest. I listen to tapes a friend back home made for me: Bach and Beethoven and Brahms, and then I listen to Al Green and bellow the lyrics of "Tired of Being Alone."

But I'm not alone. I'm meeting people. A couple I met at a Leo Kottke concert invited me for dinner and yes, dinner was all creamed this and fried that and yes, dessert was Jell-O with Dream Whip and yes, when we went for a walk after dinner and I picked up a fossil on the mountain path and made the mistake of marveling about evolution, everyone went silent, and No, I will not be going back for another dinner but they were kind people and I was grateful for their hospitality. My colleagues at the university have extended themselves, despite the fact that most of them know I was hired for more money than they are making, and they have had me over for spaghetti and jug wine and long hilarious porch-told anecdotes about Mr. Faulkner and Miss Welty delivered in brilliant, well-timed drawls. My MFA students have invited me to join them for beers after class. Gomer has asked me for coffee. So, it's not the people here. It's me. "You're too self-conscious," the professor who hired me said at a party one night. He was a big man, drunk, and I had to step back from his jabbing forefinger. "You'll never fit in." Good, I thought at the time. But today I feel lonely.

Heading back into Fayetteville at twilight I decide to drive up Mt. Sequoyah to see the sunset. I park by the huge silver cross on Skyline and get out. The sunset is gold and red and orange, staining the entire western horizon. If I could, I'd fly in one straight line over Oklahoma, Texas, New Mexico, Arizona, I'd soar home over the Golden Gate, which I can almost see—almost—as the light fades then disappears.

An old man with a little white dog walks up the hill, stops to study my California license plate, and smiles. "Welcome to Arkansas," he says, his voice soft and amused.

It takes me a moment before I can smile back. I cannot imagine anyone from San Francisco welcoming someone with Arkansas plates. "Thank you," I say at last. "I'm glad to be here."

2000

This is the best year of my life. So why, about to return to Fayetteville after a successful weekend spent publicizing *Iron Shoes* in the Bay Area, am I parked at a gas station in Corte Madera peering under the seat of my rental car? How could I have lost my wallet? I need to be at SFO in two hours to catch the last plane to XNA, but I can't drive to the airport without my wallet. I can't pay for the rental car without my credit card. And I certainly can't get on a plane without my ID or ticket. So where is the damn thing? It's not inside the car. I've checked every crevice. Did it fall to the ground when I got out to see which side the gas tank was on? Of course! It must have! I struggle out of the car again, pace around backward, forward, and finally lower myself to the ground, my nylons snagging on the rough concrete, my palms gritty, to look under the chassis. No.

Maybe someone turned it in. The turbaned man at the register inside the station shakes his head. No? Impossible! It can't—I laugh, incredulous—have just disappeared! My big red wallet. Wait! Did I leave it back at the ATM in Fairfax, fifteen minutes away? I had it there. Didn't I? I withdrew one hundred dollars. Didn't I? Heart racing, scared, furious at myself, I return to the car, barrel back the way I came, park in a disabled zone, and rush into the bank.

Has anyone turned in a wallet? The tellers shake their heads and the customers in line turn around to stare at my disheveled clothes and flushed face. Go to the police station, I am advised. Someone might have turned it in there. The police station is three blocks away. The uniformed woman at the desk hasn't seen it but offers to type up a form that might at least get me on the plane. I sink onto a wooden bench while she types, my head in my hands. The things I have lost in this life! The coin purses and shoulder bags and passports and Visa cards. The cash. The addresses, the library books, the letters, the friends—the lovers—the dogs! My mother's emerald tennis bracelet. Dan's wedding ring. That little gold Chinese coin that Miss Buck gave me when I was seven; my laptop! Stolen from the unlocked trunk of a car I'd parked at Diamond Head! With all my manuscripts in it! That was the worst. But this is almost as bad. I will be late getting back to my classes, I will lose my job, my savings, my house; I will be plunged into debt, homeless, alone.

"Here you go," the policewoman says, handing me a typed form and adding, despite the fact that she is at least twenty years younger than I, a quiet: "Don't cry." Crying, I thank her, tuck the form inside my purse, and head back to the highway. Approaching the gas station in Corte Madera again, I wipe my eyes, stop, and decide to check once more. The man behind the register reaches under the counter and hands me a big red packet which shimmers, eerie, as if not real.

"A deaf man turned it in," he says. An angel, I think. I open it up. The one hundred dollars are gone, but my credit cards, driver's license, and plane tickets are safe inside. All the way across the bridge to the city I keep my hand on my wallet. My heart does not stop racing and my lips do not stop moving in prayer. Once again, for no good reason, I have been saved. I owe Someone Something and I need to atone. I will start, I decide, by thanking the kind policewoman. But when I look for her letter later, I can't find it. Not in my purse, not in my pocket, nowhere.

2001

I follow the directions to Beaver Lake, take a series of unpaved roads to a clearing above a cliff, park, stop to admire the sunset over the water, then gather my jacket and a bottle of red wine, and pick my way down a leaf-littered dirt trail to the cabin. I hear laughter and guitar music as I approach the cabin but am stopped cold by the sight of a skinned doe hanging head down and gutted off the branch of a birch tree. She looks murdered. God, I think, what am I doing in Arkansas? I almost turn back but Mike comes out just then, joint in one hand, jelly jar of whiskey in the other, and waves me in, eager to tell me how he tracked the doe through the woods that morning and shot her with one arrow—his brown eyes bright behind grandpa glasses, his words slow-tumbling over each other, his laugh a boyish gulp. Mike is a tall, rumple-haired, big-eared man who hosts a popular radio show and gives house concerts in Fayetteville. He is rumored to have slept with every woman in town, which seems unlikely to me for he always looks half asleep and is not that attractive. He introduces me to the other guests, a guitarist, a songwriter, and a bass player, and then goes outside to barbecue the "best venison ya'll will ever eat."

"How do you know Mike?" the guitarist asks after I confess that this will be the *first* venison I will ever eat. I explain that I don't know Mike; I just met him through a friend. The guitarist and the songwriter look at each other. "Be careful," they say.

Or do they? Is it just that everyone else will soon be saying the same thing that I think they say it too? I drive back in the dark that night, humming "Gardenia Waltz," Mike's warm drawl in my ear. He's always been fixin' to come to San Francisco, he told me, has always wanted to see the Golden Gate Bridge. Maybe someday I'll show him around? In the meantime, maybe I'd like to take a boat ride out on the lake with him this weekend?

2002

Holly Smith weaves down the aisle of the Airporter straight toward me. Holly is a tall, silver-haired, Harvard-educated Dean of Medicine at UCSF. I had pretended not to see him when I boarded; I had made a big show of struggling with my carry-on, and I had prayed he would not see me at least until we arrived at SFO and I could make a dash for the gate to Fayetteville. No luck. Holly balances down the aisle of the bus like the star athlete he once was, swift, graceful, unstoppable. One large hand lands on my shoulder, the other dangles dangerously near my tightly clasped laptop. It will be all right, I tell myself. I didn't do anything wrong.

"I read your novel," Holly says.

Silence. *Iron Shoes* came out two years ago. "Zesty prose" one reviewer said; "sparkling and witty." But I know Holly does not want to talk about my zesty prose. He wants to talk about my characters, the daughter, who is based on me, only nicer, and the parents, who are based on my parents, only meaner, and the plot, which is roughly about divorce, depression, and death with a soupçon of alcoholism, addiction, and possible incest thrown in for good measure.

"You weren't writing about Jack and Dori, were you?" Holly asks.

"Mom and Dad?" I parrot brightly. "No!"

Holly waits.

I clear my throat and look out the window. The bus descends the grade and heads into the tunnel leading to the Golden Gate Bridge. Inside the tunnel, traffic slows, and then, to my horror, stalls. Above us, the tunnel darkens.

"Were you?" Holly repeats.

"No," I croak again.

"I hope not," Holly says. "Because…"

At UCSF, Holly is fondly and unironically known as Doctor God. He and his wife Margaret had lived next door to my parents for years; they were close friends. Holly thought my dad was "a sweet man"—that was the phrase he used at the funeral—and he thought my mother was "a little darling." He could not imagine a more attractive, spirited, glamorous couple. "So much fun to be with."

"Because," Holly says, "I loved them."

And they loved him. Dad, sarcastic about everyone else, was awed by Holly's accomplishments, his brilliance, humility, and humor. Mom loved Holly because he was handsome and kind and he always checked up on her during her many amputations. After the cancer went to her brain, Mom hallucinated about him. "Jack," she would call from the bed, her voice plaintive, "Holly wants a dish of gelato. Would you please serve Holly a dish of strawberry gelato?" and Dad, looking up from his crossword puzzle, would shout toward the bedroom, "No one is here, Doris."

"He wants strawberry, Jack. Is that asking too much? Would you please just get Holly a simple dish of strawberry gelato?"

Instead of rising, as I would have, to pantomime scooping invisible gelato into an invisible bowl and offering it to a column of empty air, Dad simply rolled his eyes, lit another cigarette, and sank down in his leather chair. He'd endured Mom losing her health, but losing her mind was killing him. He remembered the morning when she'd turned to him and announced she was going on a journey and would be leaving soon, and since then he often asked when. "Oh, I've changed my mind about all that," Mom would answer, emaciated and calm. "I'm not going anywhere. I'm staying right here."

An hour later, when the Smiths did drop by to see her, Mom hadn't recognized them; she thought Margaret was a sorority sister from her college days who had married a giant, and cattily remarked after they left how fat she had gotten.

"You made those parents up," Holly prompts now. "Right?"

"Totally," I babble, sounding like one of my students. "Everyone in the book is totally made up."

"Because they sure didn't sound like the Jack and Doris I knew."

"Of course not. Not at all." I mean, I almost say: how could they? The parents in my novel were cruel to their children, two-faced to their friends, casually hateful to each other. They were the parents I knew. But they were not the parents Holly knew, or needed to know.

"It's fiction," I explain. "Of course, I may have used parts of…you know, here and there…"

"They enjoyed their Scotch," Holly concedes. "But that scene with the morphine?"

"Fiction!"

"And the dog?"

Was there a dog in the book? I can't remember! Is he tricking me? Holly doesn't trick people. I take a chance, shake my head vigorously and insist again. "Fiction!"

Holly's eyes are luminous in the tunnel's dusk. I honestly can't tell if he believes me or not. He may not be used to lies. His own children, grown now into admirable adults, all six working for the benefit of humanity in the fields of poverty law, science, and education, have never, to my knowledge, lied.

"Well," he says, straightening to his full height, "I miss them. Your folks."

"I miss them too," I admit.

"Then perhaps you'll write another book soon."

"Yes. Good. I mean to."

The bus groans, lurches, and starts up again. Holly removes his hand from my shoulder and walks back to his seat. We move slowly forward. The cold winter light falls on my hot cheeks through the window as we exit the tunnel, accelerate and rumble onto the span. I lean back, exhausted.

I remember the accounts I've read of near-death experiences—souls plummeting through dark tunnels just like this one only to emerge into light and the welcoming arms of their dear departed. I imagine Mom greeting me with her heavy silver hairbrush raised, ready to strike, and Dad turned aside, thoughtfully fingering a putting iron. Welcome to the afterlife, kid.

I smile, sour. I deserve their wrath. I know I betrayed them. But tough. I'm a writer. That's what writers do. I had to tell the truth, didn't I? If I was unkind to my parents, they were unkind to me; if I was unfair, so be it. I told my life story the same way they used to tell their life stories, and for the same reasons: for shock effect, for attention, for laughs, and, face it (Mom's favorite phrase), for pity. You made me what I am, I mouth to the empty air. And, I add, finally giving Holly what he'd wanted all along, I am really, really sorry.

2003

Sometimes I think I *am* this damn bridge.

My Better Self leans forward in the passenger seat, ready, as always, for a fight. *What do you mean?*

Stalled. Stuck. Not going anywhere.

My Better Self nods at the two-lane Friday night crush to San Francisco that has forced us to a crawl. *It gets worse every year,* she agrees. *But you're referring to traffic here, not the bridge. The bridge itself isn't stalled. If you are going to milk a metaphor, you should be more precise. What makes you think you are the bridge?*

I'm supporting everyone.

What are you talking about? Your daughters are grown and doing well. Gretchen has happily remarried and is editing a weekly newspaper; Rachel is teaching at Utrecht University; Devon is in law school. Your parents are gone. Your dog is gone. Your two twenty-one-year-old cats finally died. Who else do you have to "support"?

I don't know. I just feel this weight on me….

Oh for heaven's sake. You're back in California as Visiting Writer at San Jose State this spring and there is no way you can complain about your workload; it's easy, and your students are a good bunch, hardly demanding. You let Ken live in your cottage when he was recovering from hip surgery, yes, but you were hardly supporting him—and as for paying for Mike's dental work and buying him a motorboat and putting up with his drunks and depressions and infidelities, well, you were warned, weren't you? Whatever made you think you two could be happy together? Just because a guy serenades you on a hand-hewn dulcimer on a rickety pier by a man-made lake in the Ozarks doesn't mean that you can build a life together. You two have nothing in common. What did he say when you asked if he considered you a Yankee? "Oh no," he said, "you're a foreigner." What did he say about the Golden Gate Bridge when you finally paid for him to fly out to visit you last month? He kept his eyes closed when you drove him over it, didn't he? He talked about himself the whole time, didn't he? Is that why you think you are the bridge—because he's never seen you either?

Well yes, and because I still hang in there. Suspended…

So break up with him! How long did you stay suspended with Ken, by the way? Fourteen years? Fifteen? And how long were you married to Dan? Twelve years? And Richard? Twelve? When will you learn?

Rusting away…

Start taking Vitamin D like you've been told to. Dust off those Jane Fonda tapes. Get back to the gym. Meditate. What happened to tai chi? I thought you were going to learn tai chi.

In need of new paint…

Less is more at your age, dearie.

Taken for granted...

Is all this because you're not writing? Why aren't you writing? It's just a question of discipline. Start getting up at five-thirty, that's easy enough, you'll have a new book before Christmas.

Strung out...

I'm not listening anymore.

Alone under an empty sky...

La la la.

Over an empty abyss...

Oh for god's sake. Get over yourself. Dump Mike before he dumps you, start writing every day, go visit Rachel in Amsterdam, take that summer job in Ireland, lose those ten pounds you've been talking about ever since you were eight years old, and get a kitten.

2004

My novel has only been out four years and already it's being remaindered? No one wants to take her home? No one wants to bed down with her? Okay, she's homely, she's clumsy, but she's sweet; she's funny; she's dear. And she's imprisoned in a warehouse? And she's going to be (I can't let myself say it) *pulped* soon?

"All you need to do," my agent says, "is write a second novel."

Oh yes. That second novel.

"Surely you have some ideas," my agent prompts.

But I don't!

My friend Susan suggests I take five people I know who do not know each other, put them in a place I know but they do not, and kill one of them.

My friend Emily suggests I write about the girl Mike just dumped after he dumped me. "She tried to kill herself," Emily says. "Can you imagine anything more embarrassing? Killing yourself for *Mike*?"

My friend Jackson suggests I write about the time he was ten years old and walking through a graveyard with his aunt when a blind fiddler passed them and his aunt said, "Do you know who that was, Jackson?" and Jackson said, "No," and she said, "That was your daddy."

My sister Bridget suggests I write about unrequited love: "You know so much about it."

My sister Nora thinks I should write about a woman whose husband after thirty years of marriage turns out to be gay, or no, she says grimly, she should write that book herself.

My therapist thinks I should write about her brother, who is having a hard time, which is one of the reasons she keeps missing her appointments with me.

Devon suggests I write a legal thriller, Rachel wonders why I write at all, and Gretchen says I can write about anything I want but I better not write about her again or she'll never speak to me again.

I nod, listening, not really connecting, until one afternoon in December, back in the Bay Area for the winter break and once again driving over the Golden Gate Bridge, it occurs to me that I can simply write about a woman like myself: a white, middle-aged, middle-class, middlebrow woman who has had four men in her life: One man is alcoholic, another penniless, one will be clinically depressed, another chronically unfaithful. The woman, out of kindness—kindness? maybe…or cowardice…I'll figure that out later—will end up caretaking all of them, bringing them into her house, putting one man in her basement, another in her attic, another in her den, another in her toolshed. None in the bedroom!

Then Something Will Happen (TBA) and ta-dum, the woman will heal the men, heal herself, and grow up!

It will be a comic novel, I decide. Lighthearted. Upbeat. It will take no time to write; it will practically write itself. I should be finished in six months! I even have the title: *The Home for Unwed Husbands*.

"Well," my agent says, her voice tentative, "I like the title..."

2005

All I've brought from Arkansas to San Francisco on this busy weekend is a chigger bite. Chiggers are unknown to San Franciscans. My luncheon mates at Moose's in North Beach listen to me with attentive frowns. "These bites last how long?" one of the women asks.

"Weeks," I assure her.

"And you can't see them?"

"Chiggers are invisible," I say, and then, showing off, "You know what an Ozark beauty bath is? Two parts water to two parts Clorox."

The women laugh. These are all accomplished, sophisticated, interesting women—artists, photographers, activists, writers. One woman has been overseeing the renovation of the de Young Museum, another has been assisting Andy Goldsworthy, another is making a film about Christo's Gates, and another is about to go to Turkey to participate in the excavation of a newly discovered city that may have been a matriarchy. They know a lot about Paris and Hanoi and Rio, but they know nothing about Arkansas, and when I show up at lunch, they quiz me.

"Are you still dating that redneck you told us about?" one of them asks. "The deer hunter with the mandolin? The fellow you said looked like he'd 'been rode hard and put up wet'?"

I shake my head. "He dumped me. I'm seeing an Irish alcoholic I met at a funeral now."

Long looks and then attention, thankfully, veers. I soon take my leave and duck into Saints Peter and Paul's in Washington Square to wait until meeting David at two. I slink into a back pew, furtively reach into my purse for the little tub of Chiggerex I brought with me, claw some out, and slap it over the burning bite on my bra line. I should go up to the altar, light a candle, and ask for forgiveness. "Do your friends and family have any idea how you describe them behind their backs?" someone once asked me.

No! No one does.

I hope.

I rise from the pew as David appears, fresh-faced, newly sober once again, a bouquet behind his back: pink roses, gray thistles, gold iris—flowers he bought on the street outside from two old sisters. He tells me about the sisters as we walk out into the sunlight and through North Beach; he knows their names, and where they lived in Hungary, and how they survived the Holocaust.

He talks steadily all afternoon, his brogue impeccable despite the fact that he has lived in the States for the last forty years. Standing two inches in front of me in City Lights bookstore, he asks if I know that the word "whiskey" comes from the Gaelic *uisce beatha* meaning "water of life"; pushing my espresso aside at Enrico's, he recounts a story about being hauled off to security in a fancy hotel simply because he told the desk clerk he needed to micturate; jostling my elbow as we cruise through the exhibit at the Legion of Honor, he tells me about his past of prisons, dead-end jobs, missions, detox centers, betrayals, knife attacks, dead friends, and AA sponsors.

He does not stop talking until we finally arrive at the San Francisco Library Laureates Dinner at the library where I am to speak tonight. We are seated in the African American room, surrounded by patrons who have paid to meet local writers and "engage them in discourse about the creative process"—thankfully, these patrons are as diverse and interesting as the women in my luncheon group, and I enjoy talking with them. David leaves my side to talk to an author at another table who wrote a bestselling book on addiction. I see him kneeling by the author's chair, talking intelligently, earnestly, relentlessly. The author tries to meet my eyes across the room, but I don't let him.

David is still talking as we begin the drive back in my rental car to Woodacre for the night. He's already gone across the bridge once this day, he tells me, and while waiting for the bus at the toll plaza, the strangest thing happened: a bicyclist pedaled up, dismounted, pointed at the sky, and said, "Oh look, my buddy is already here, waiting for me." David looked up and saw a big black crow. "Bet he wants a peanut," the bicyclist said, and he pulled a peanut from his pocket and threw it straight up into the air. The crow snapped it up and flew away. "Now look," the bicyclist said, "his brother wants one." Again, the man tossed a peanut into the sky and a second crow snapped it up in midair.

"That's a wonderful story," I start to say, but David interrupts, takes my hand, kisses it, and starts to recite, "Shall I compare thee to a summer's day," which worked pretty well when I heard it for the first time, less well the second, third, and fourth times. We will be together all weekend. Can I stand it? He's a sweet man. I'll try. I free my hand to scratch my chigger bite.

2006

"Homesick for the Bay Area?" Jim gives me his sunny, gap-toothed smile. I have run into him at the Lowe's Garden Center in Fayetteville; we are both holding potted Easter lilies, on sale, the week after Easter. "You should come visit me in Beaver."

"What's in Beaver?"

"Your bridge."

I wait, puzzled.

"The Little Golden Gate. You've heard of it?"

"No."

Jim's smile widens. He is a retired dean of religious studies at the university and the mayor of Beaver, a town forty minutes north of Fayetteville, population under one hundred. I met him at a book reading in town last year and we have since gone out for coffee once or twice; he is slightly older than I, divorced, with an ex-wife who won't speak to him and five grown children scattered throughout the country. He is tall and handsome but—it has to be said—a little too nice for me. He attends the Christian Science church and he runs a monthly metaphysical discussion group I avoid.

"It's a replica of the real Golden Gate, of course," he explains. "But it's a genuine suspension bridge, the only one left in Arkansas. You might want to check it out whenever you need a California fix. I know how you must get sometimes"—he peers at me kindly—"lonely."

Lonely? Yes. There are nights here in Fayetteville when I feel that mean stab. But not often. Paloma, an arrogant cross-eyed Siamese kitten I picked up at the shelter, is a kick, perverse and playful, and she's been great company. My sister Bridget and her husband have retired to a lake house in the next state and she and I spend Thanksgivings together and meet for giggly barbecued rib pig-outs in Eureka Springs, an old Victorian spa town that reminds us both somehow of growing up in Mill Valley. I drive out to the country on Thursdays to play Scrabble with a group of bluegrass musicians; they are all excellent Scrabble players and chortle as they tally their phenomenal scores, repeating, "So you teach English at the university?" Once a month the Ladies Lounge meets to discuss topics like Menopause or Mothers or Menopausal Mothers, and we share a potluck and exchange life stories. On Sunday mornings I have lavish brunches with a group of intelligent, spirited, open-minded women I met through our mutual poet friend Brenda, and on Sunday afternoons I meet with Patty and Kathleen and Boujie and Paul and Carolyn and Charles and Enid at Ellen's house, where we sit around a long table, snack on decaf coffee and dry Cheerios, and read Shakespeare plays out loud without pausing for footnotes or explanations, just throwing ourselves into the narrative. "Don't forget," Ellen reminds us, taking her seat at the head of the table, "I'm the king," and though I am usually a lesser Lady or Second Murderer, and though all of us read extremely poorly, still, sitting in a lovely room listening to someone drawl "Aught aught damn spaught" feels as close to Sunday services as I suspect I'll ever get.

Then too, there are the AA meetings. I don't like going to these meetings and I don't go often. I am ashamed to be there; I'd never want my daughters or friends or students or colleagues to know I go. I am the last to arrive, the first to leave, and I never speak. It doesn't matter that I've never had a car accident or lost a job or that the outward demonstrations of my addiction are minor compared to the horror stories related by the Vietnam vets and disbarred lawyers and bruised wives who call themselves "real drunks." I know what I am and I don't want anyone else to know. I listen to everyone else's "shares" politely; I read the Big Book, memorize the Steps, and mouth the prayers. I don't believe any of it, but one of the things I like about AA is that I don't have to believe it; I just have to not drink. And AA has made that easier to do.

"Call me," Jim says.

"I will," I promise, but of course I don't, and it is not until many months later that my new GPS misguides me back from a reading in Eureka Springs and I emerge from a dark pine forest to find myself approaching a pretty toy structure with two yellow towers spanning a river. I slow. This must be the bridge.

Seeing that it's one lane only, I hold my breath and start forward, aware of the wooden planks creaking beneath my wheels. It only takes a few minutes to reach the other side; once there I park on the tree-shaded bank and look back. This little bridge is actually sort of darling. No tolls. Clearly no suicides—children could safely jump off the rails, at least when the river is low.

I wonder if I should call Jim to thank him. But then I remember that Jim has recently had a huge spiritual break-through. He has started receiving messages from God and he has been posting them on Facebook and sending them out in weekly newsletters. The messages are benign enough—*Love Means Being True To The Inner Truth Of Your Being*, etc. They are punctuated with exclamation marks, and although they aren't that much different from the slogans I hear in AA meetings, they are not for me. I start the car and drive on.

2007

The vows have been made, the cake has been cut, the toasts have been given, and all three of my daughters are out on the dance floor. Gretchen is sexily twirling with her second husband; Rachel, in a brown business suit, is demurely two-stepping with two-year-old Kai; Devon is radiant in the arms of her young groom.

"It must feel good," someone says. "To see them all grown up."

"Yes," I lie. "Very good."

"You must be proud."

"Oh," and this is the truth, "I had nothing to do with how well they've turned out."

I try to smile, fail, excuse myself, and turn to find Richard. So far, my ex-husband has behaved like a prince. He arrived on time for the ceremony, beautifully dressed in a new gray suit; he led Devon down the grassy aisle to the flower-strewn wedding arch without missing a step; he nodded to Ken, who, leaning on a cane, gravely nodded back; he gave me a check for his share of the expenses; and he brought a nice date, an ophthalmologist named Jimmy. After years of volunteer work in Persian and Oriental carpet stores, he's been hired to work in an elegant gallery in Pacific Heights; he now flies on buying trips to New York City and delivers orders to Bill Gates. He seems to be happy. But you can't trust Richard. He has a tendency to disappear and his moods, at least when he's drinking, go up and down. I am not surprised to find him sitting alone at a far table, crying.

"Isn't it sad?" he says, when I come up.

"Weddings? Yes. I hate them."

"No, I mean about Bonnie."

"My brother's wife Bonnie?"

"I can't believe she died."

"She died years ago, Richard. Danny's here today with his new wife."

Richard, unconsoled, bows his head. He lives in the past even more than I do, and I look around for his friend Jimmy, but Jimmy seems to have left. Ken is chatting with a bridesmaid. My sister Bridget smokes in a corner, shivering in a jacket she has borrowed from a stranger; she has forgotten how cold it is in California. My sister Nora sits quietly holding hands with her beautiful daughter Nell, who, undergoing chemo, is wearing a wig. My brother Dan, one arm around his young wife, raises his voice to wonder again why Devon and her groom chose to celebrate the holy sacrament of marriage outdoors in Tilden Park instead of in a real church. The groom's father and mother chat with their guests from Orange County, and Devon's law-school friends clown around the dance floor, high on something a lot stronger than champagne.

I leave Richard to his grief and escape to the patio. I have my own grief, and it makes no more sense than his. I have always confused weddings with funerals and all I can think of today is how bereft I feel. It's not that I am losing Devon—she is twenty-eight, after all, a practicing attorney—and she was never "mine" to "lose" in the first place. All of my daughters are undeserved gifts. I know that. Whatever I'm feeling today has nothing to do with my children.

For the seventieth time I wish I still smoked. For the eightieth time, I wish I still drank. I yearn to find my car, crawl inside, lock the doors, solve a crossword puzzle and ditch everyone, the way Dad used to. Dad is dead, Mom is dead, I have no lover, the new novel I'm (still) writing is a mess, my life has been one long string of failures, and my mother-of-the-bride dress with its little chiffon capelet is so hideous I cannot wait to tear it off and throw it in the Goodwill bag. Tomorrow I will have to pack and make the long trek over the bridge and back to SFO and Fayetteville and my classes again: back and forth, back and forth, that's all my life is these days, back and forth, going nowhere.

"Mother?" Rachel at my elbow, Kai still in her arms, four-year-old Annika beside her. "Are you all right?"

"No." I reach down to rearrange the flower girl wreath on Annika's tangled hair. "Dance with Oma?" I ask her.

Annika grins, shouts "*Nee*," in her shrill Dutch voice, and scampers off to corral her latest love, the best man, an ex-Olympian who knows how to twirl her around until she screams with delight. Screams of delight are not Oma's specialty, never have been, never will be. I realize I am about to cry.

"Mother?"

"I just don't understand why you had to move all the way to the Netherlands," I say. I wipe my eyes. "And I really think Annika should be taught to say 'No, thank you' in proper English."

"She can say No any way she wants to," Rachel snaps back.

Devon steps out to the patio, brightens at the sight of the two of us glaring at each other, and glides forward, arms outstretched, graceful, regal, serene in her white satin sheath. "This is the happiest day of my life," she says, giving us both a light hug. I am gratified to catch a whiff of sweat under all her perfumes before she glides away. So today is hard for her too? No. Of course it isn't. This is my problem, this grief, this loneliness, or envy, or whatever it is. Oh. Self-pity?

Gretchen, flushed and gorgeous, shimmies up to Rachel and me, and puts her arms around both our waists. "Devon is going to have a perfect life," she predicts.

"Really?" I pull back. Why can't I stop myself? I yank a tissue out of the sleeve of my horrible dress and blow my nose. "A perfect life? She works with rapists and sex offenders at the courthouse all day. Her honeymoon is going to be spent on a golf course. Her in-laws don't believe in global warming."

"*Mother*," both girls chorus.

Richard finds me at the end of the afternoon. Devon has left; Gretchen has left; Rachel has left; and, drunk, Richard says, "I still love you, you know, I always have, I think about us getting together again all the time."

I listen with satisfaction. This is actually very good to hear and I am touched. For a moment I am even tempted. But does Richard truly live in the past? Doesn't he remember that we were a terrible couple? For the last two years of our marriage Richard lay on the couch watching golf matches, one hand over his mouth and the other over his crotch, while I paced around him, snarling. When I asked what was wrong, he said "Nothing," and gave one of those low groans that always set my teeth on edge—though once, I remember, he added a Richard-ism that almost made me fall for him all over again: "My libido's incognito."

"It would take a lot of work," I point out.

He groans.

"We'd have to get to know each other all over again. We'd have to talk, for starters. We've never talked. We don't know how. We'd have to go to therapy."

He groans again.

"Look, why don't you come visit me next month in Arkansas? We can spend a few days together and…"

"I can't take a vacation right now."

"Well, the month after, then."

Silence.

"You could bring your friend Jimmy."

"Why would I want to bring Jimmy?"

"I don't know. It was just an idea. You brought him to the wedding."

"Oh babe, I'm just so sorry we ever split up."

Twenty-two years ago, I think. Best thing that ever happened to either one of us. Still, I rest my head on his shoulder. It's been a long time since anyone's called me babe.

2008

Deborah has a weak bladder, low blood sugar, needs to eat dinner at 5:30, do an hour of yoga every day, and be in bed by eight o'clock. Sweet-tempered and cheerful, but always too cold, too hot, or too hungry, she has been our baby on this trip to Spain. Anne, frowning over the maps and train schedules, is our mom. I'm the same stray dog I've always been; I should be on a leash. Because I had my purse stolen in Barcelona an hour after I arrived, I follow my two friends with one hand pressed to my money belt; I have to race to catch up every time they turn a corner.

We have clambered around the squiggly cartoon chimneys on the roof of Sagrada Família, strolled the theatrical length of Las Ramblas, spent hours in the Prado, shopped the Christmas markets of the Plaza Mayor, rented a car and driven to Toledo (neither Deborah nor Anne even suggested I drive), marveled at the mosque in Córdoba, slept in chilly paradors, peered at prehistoric paintings on dank cave walls in Ronda and now here we are in a large hotel in Sevilla on New Year's Eve—and while it is too early perhaps to say

Sevilla is my favorite place in the world, it already comes close. The scent of the city alone—orange trees, coffee, slaughterhouses, and diesel—intoxicates me, and I am no longer annoyed at Deborah for being sleepy nor at Anne for reminding me to look where I'm going.

Still, it's a long wait for midnight. We have finished our pizzas, Mars bars, and Perrier; we have written our postcards and read our books; at one point, I turn the television on, and we watch a few minutes of *Vertigo*—the scene where Kim Novak, fully dressed, leaps into the Bay beneath the bridge at Fort Point.

"Dan and I used to park down there and make out," I remember, as I turn the set off, and my friends look at me blankly, not sure who Dan is. "Gretchen and Rachel's father," I explain. "Before your time." They nod. We three have known each other for years but we don't know everything. I knew Deborah's husband before he divorced her, remarried her, and died. I knew Anne's third husband (not the first two) and am not surprised when I hear he still begs her to come over and cook dinner for him and his new wife. I never hear from Dan anymore—his wife doesn't like us to talk—and I haven't seen or heard from Richard since Devon's wedding when he suggested we get back together. David still leaves long lilting monologues on my answering machine, and Ken and I meet for breakfast once or twice a year (I pay). I think of Mike almost every day with an ache I cannot understand, for of all the men I've ever loved, Mike is the least plausible partner, and the one I should forget.

At 11:30, Anne puts down her Sudoku and says, "You know what? I'm going to quit working at the gallery. I'm too good for it. Plus, I'm underpaid." She points at me. "What are you under?"

"A deadline," I say.

"What are you under, Deborah?" Anne calls, and Deborah, who has napped all afternoon in preparation for this late night and is now doing headstands in the doorway, says: "A lucky star."

Anne and I look at each other and laugh, for it's true, then the three of us join the thousands of revelers on the Plaza Nueva. We each have our paper packet of twelve green grapes and, following what we've been told is the Spanish custom, pop one into our mouths for luck each time the bell tolls. Soon it will be midnight and I'm praying that 2009 will finally be my year, the year I finish *The Home for Unwed Husbands*, learn Spanish, retire from teaching, sell my Fayetteville house, move back to Woodacre, and find a good man. I glance at my friends. They've no idea that I am secretly celebrating my third year of sobriety tonight, nor do they know what I would give, at this moment, for a bottle of cheap Spanish red and a dark place to drink it in.

2009

Fear of ice storms. Fear of thunder. Fear of failing. Fear of mother. Fear of travel. Fear of theft. Fear of falling. Fear of death. Fear of teaching—public speaking. Fear of phone. Fear of flu. Fear of drought. Fear of you. Fear of day. Fear of night. Fear of depths, fear of heights...

Wait. Okay? Hold it. Fear of heights? Are you saying that you have never actually walked across this Golden Gate Bridge you've been going on and on about for all these pages? No? You haven't? And you never will? You never will because you're terrified? Do you think you are entitled to write about something you have been too terrified to experience yourself? Something you know nothing about?

Fear of voices, fear of deadlines, fear of choices, fear of headlines. Fear of never getting a second look. Fear of never finishing this fucking book. Fear of anger, fear of hate, and yes. Okay? Fear of walking across the Golden Gate.

2010

One of the writers I mentor has been working on her new novel for four years now and it isn't done yet. Her agent is anxious, her publisher is impatient, and she and I are sick of each other. I have become a scold and she a careless girl with better things to do. She shrugs "Me bad" when I nag and that makes me nag more. It's not as if I am doing any better with my own book—"The Home" gets worse with every revision and so far, not a single reader I've shown it to has liked it. *I* don't like it. And yet I keep stubbornly at it, hoping some inexplicable magic will kick in. Is it just ego? It would be so nice to have a second novel to claim. I know I don't want to die like my mother did, with a bunch of rumpled pages jammed into a box and the words "I'm so frustrated" on my lips. But...do I want to be known as the author of these (so far) seven sodden revisions?

My mentee has problems far worse than mine, for her novel—her fifth or sixth—has already been sold and her public is holding hungry hands out. Setting schedules hasn't worked, insisting on homework hasn't worked, foretelling disaster hasn't worked. What *does* seem to work is something I learned about when I taught in Hawaii years ago: talk story.

Talk story is easy. Talk story is fun. The mentee and I can sprawl on her living room couch in the middle of a sunny afternoon with our teacups and gossip about characters no one has ever heard about but us. We can debate their fates on the telephone. With her husband at the wheel driving back from dinner in the city one night, we can wonder if so and so should keep her fortune or throw it away, or if such and such happened in a spring snowstorm or a winter thaw and whether he or she should ride over a bridge like this in a motorcycle or sail beneath it in a boat or fly over it with a lover—or a villain—who hasn't been invented yet, but could be, could have just arrived from Paris or Moscow or Mars. I offer prompt after prompt and the mentee, who is effortlessly inventive, responds with idea after idea, some of them absurd, some of them brilliant, our voices tumbling over each other and our laughter ringing out like children's laughter for we are both remembering that we *are* children, and that writing, after all, is play.

2011

I love my West Coast Literature class. I get to talk about my favorite books, most of which my Arkansas students have never heard of: *Fat City, So Long, Woman Warrior, Rachel at the Wedding, Yellow Back Radio Broke-Down, Women in Their Beds, Mrs. Bridge, East of Eden, Play It as It Lays, Jesus' Son...* am I working my MFA students too hard? Am I giving them too much to read? They can take it. They are an attentive, bright, and gifted group. They almost make me want to continue teaching.

Almost. For I never meant to teach in the first place. I was happy enough working as a secretary for those seven psycho psychiatrists years ago—that job gave me time to write, at least. The way I ended up taking over my graduate class at San Francisco State was a fluke—the professor, whose name I no longer remember, became ill and the Chair tapped me to step in and finish the semester. How frightened I was that first day, trembling before the class in a leather vest and red cowboy boots, mispronouncing names, laughing at my own jokes, handing back single-spaced typed responses that were often longer than the student's story my response was critiquing. I never expected to be rehired the following fall. But somehow, I was. And somehow, I taught there for the next seventeen years, unsteadily advancing from adjunct to assistant to associate to full tenured professor until Arkansas recruited me to teach in Fayetteville.

I'm a better teacher now than I was thirty years ago. Not as nervous anyway, not as uncertain. I've learned—though I often forget—that the secret to teaching is love. You have to love your subject and you have to love your students. Most of the time, I can manage both. But tonight, as I leave my office and walk across the campus back to my car, I'm thinking it's time to quit. Teaching creative writing has been a sham job all along anyway, hasn't it? I've never known what creative writing is—isn't all writing creative?—nor have I believed for one instant it can be taught. Learned, yes. But taught? Not by me, anyway. I've never believed that fiction can be graphed in a neat series of rising arcs. I don't know what an unreliable narrator is. Aren't they all unreliable? I don't understand the end of most stories and I don't enjoy tearing them apart. I would rather gossip about an author's personal life than look at how he handles point of view. I don't use PowerPoint. I don't show movies. And I am getting more emotional. Last week in my undergraduate class I started to cry. The students didn't like *Death in Venice*. They thought it was boring. Boring? I opened the book at random and read a page out loud to prove to them that it wasn't boring, it was beautiful, and the page I read *was* beautiful and my voice broke and the tears came, and there I stood, an old lady weeping in front of a roomful of horrified sophomores. I understood then that I need to quit, and quit soon.

But maybe not today. I pause outside my car to look up at the Arkansas sunset, another nightly showcase of splendid pastels, and think about the changing sea light of San Francisco from the Ferlinghetti poem I plan to teach in my West Coast Lit class tomorrow. I miss the sea.

2012

A sunny May day, San Francisco white and bright before me, the Bay waters gray below, the tangerine crab claw colors of the bridge above me. I am driving to Leo's flat for lunch, careening up and down and through Divisadero, into Noe Valley, and onto leafy, bumpy Chattanooga Street. I park in front of his two-story Victorian, both saddened and relieved to see a cable lift has been installed on his front stairs: at least he can get in and out now, with assistance. His Filipina helper Eden answers when I ring; flushed and mussed, she shoos me inside, takes the bag of deli food I've brought, and follows me up to the landing, muttering to herself. Leo, leaning on his cane, as always wants a lip kiss and I am unable to turn my face away in time. The flat is stuffy, smells of cat, and the dining room is unlit. Eden disappears into the kitchen to unwrap the sandwiches and shake the potato chips into a bowl. She pours tea and plops plates down for us, then arranges Leo's pills in a row in front of him.

"Swallow them now," she says. "Before you eat." She raises her voice. "I said swallow them now!" She turns to me, hands on hips. "Deafer and deafer."

"Bossier and bossier," Leo corrects, ducking when she strikes his shoulder. One of his cheeks is pink, as if he'd just awakened, and there are granules of white on his lids, but he tells me he went to Pilates that morning and is feeling good, considering, he adds, that he is going to be 88 next week. He's recently had a recurrence of prostate cancer and is being treated for congestive heart failure; his ankles are arthritic, and he's having trouble with his right hand, which the doctors think might be nerve damage. His daughter still gives him grief: she has just been fired from her last acting job, and she still blames him for her childhood. One of his best friends is on the short list for the Nobel Prize in literature; another friend just died. His obese cat has an eye infection and Eden has to wrap its sharp claws in a towel while he administers the salve. Eden herself has been…well, what's the word?…sassy, Leo decides. Sassy in the shower.

"But enough of that," he finishes. "How are you doing, darling?"

I'm not ready to tell him how I'm doing yet so I say again how much I enjoyed his reading at Books Inc. the week before. Leo was wonderful, calm, commanding, dignified, reading passages from his new novel in his measured way, and then talking about Detroit, where the novel is set and where he'd grown up. The audience was packed with his friends and ex-students, and when he referred to this novel as his last book a woman in the front row quickly corrected him: "Your *latest* book," she said.

Leo nods as I remind him of this, but says, quietly, "Well, it may well be my last one," and then repeats, "In any event, darling, how are *you* doing."

I take a deep breath and tell him about the flurry of rejections I've received on my writing from Counterpoint, Sarabande, Ecco, Algonquin, Tin House, and Upstreet. I did win second prize in a little chapbook contest for my flash fiction pieces and I am, I tell him, dedicating that chapbook to him when, or if, it comes out next year. I am finally retiring—next fall will be my last term at the university; I plan to sell my house in Fayetteville and move back to my old house in Woodacre, which I have been renting out for the last thirteen years. My agent has asked me to revise *The Home for Unwed Husbands* for the umpteenth time, but I'm not sure I want to. Frankly, I am not sure I even want to be a writer anymore. I went to a literary magazine's cocktail party the other night and I was the only person over forty in the room; the refreshments consisted of popcorn and jelly beans and shots of tequila. I have a collapsed spine, osteoporosis, sciatica, and an arthritic wedding ring finger, and I had a dream the other night that I was dangling from a helicopter holding my mother by one hand, terrified to let her go. My daughters and grandchildren are fine, I'm not drinking, and I've survived a brief, unsatisfactory affair with a sarcastic Texan that ended well. I'm alone now, and I like it.

"So that's me," I conclude and rise to go. Leo reaches for another kiss. I bend down, reluctant, and brush his hand away from my breast with my elbow.

"Oh," he says, crooning my name, "I have such a strong feeling for you."

"I too, for you," I demur as I back away.

All the drive back to Marin I feel like shit. I can't forgive myself. It's true I love Leo. There have been times in my life when Leo was the only man in the world I could talk to. His honesty, warmth, intelligence, and common sense helped me through the defection and death of my father. He stood by me when I divorced Richard, and when I broke off with Ken. He always supported my teaching, laughed at my jokes, and praised my writing. He listens attentively to my whining. But why do I let him kiss me? He must know I don't like it. Why aren't I firmer? And what is going on with him and Eden? "Sassy"? In the shower? Do they take showers together? Isn't eighty-eight too old for that? So much about people I do not understand!

I go to the library to finish working on a student's manuscript. A ripe-smelling homeless man settles into the carrel next to me and chuckles as he turns the pages of a magazine. When he gets up to leave, I glance over and see that he has been reading *People*. The page on top is open to photos of Angelina Jolie and Brad Pitt. Are they finally getting married? Adopting another child? Has she made up with her father? I reach over and bring the magazine to my carrel, freezing when I hear the homeless man return and sink back into his chair. Furtively, I hide *People* under my student's manuscript and write "awkward" in the margin of one of her pages.

2013

"You must be soooooo glad to be home again!"

Am I? I'm not sure yet. I may be in culture shock. The first gas station I saw when I bumped into California on I-40 offered free massage and had a bathroom scale in the women's lavatory. The gas cost almost a dollar more a gallon than it did in Fayetteville. Tumbleweeds blew across the road as I drove up Highway Five, and I had to breathe through my mouth to deflect the rank stench of cow manure billowing out from the enormous feed lots. Coming into the Bay Area, I saw long strands of litter tangled in among the poppies on the roadside. Homeless people were camped in the shelter of the overpasses, litter blowing everywhere. The billboards along the freeways advertised Sexual Reassignment Surgeons and asked Have You Been Checked for Syphilis Lately? Approaching Marin, I was astonished not just at the uniform number of Priuses with Obama bumper stickers, but at the rudeness of the drivers; Arkansas drivers, with Bibles and pistols in their glove compartments, were far more courteous. Stopping for groceries, I marveled that my local supermarket had as many aisles for liquor as it had for produce. My cart had a cup holder for coffee, the paper coffee cup was printed with ads for Charles Schwab Investments, the coffee cost four dollars, and my bill came to $60.72 for cat food, bread, milk, and a bag of apples. At Trader Joe's checkout stand the clerk said, "Have a nice day," to the man ahead of me, the sort of pleasant thing clerks said at the IGA in Fayetteville all the time, but instead of saying, "You too," the man, tall, tanned, wearing a gold watch and spotless tennis whites, only picked up his bottle of vitamin water, shook his head, and sighed, "I'll try."

Moving back into my old house was disorienting as well. The 300-year-old oak tree I loved had fallen through the roof the summer before, and although the insurance had covered most of the repairs, the house looked forlorn without it. Having been rented out to different families for so long, the hardwood floors were scratched, the walls dented, the cupboards unhinged. The garden, which the last tenants had kept bright and cheery with enough plastic flowers to fill a cemetery, was dead. Everything was fixable, I knew that, but still I felt overwhelmed, not just by the money the repairs were going to cost, but by the memories that ambushed me in every empty room. I mourned my long-dead dog, the way Almond Joy's toenails clicked over the hardwood floors. I missed the dinner parties I used to give and the writing groups by the fireplace and the cigarettes stolen down by the creek. I missed the children! Where was the sturdy toddler, the schoolgirl in her too-short uniform, the sullen beauty who slammed in and out of doors? Instead, I had these tall, competent, intelligent beauties who laughed quietly with each other as they helped unpack my boxes. I recognized them, in a way, better than I recognized myself. Was I really this woman who got into the shower with her glasses on, left the car engine running all night, and couldn't lift her one-year-old grandson? Were these really my neighborhood friends? These handsome, toned, youthful, *New Yorker*-reading women arriving with bouquets of fresh flowers and enormous radishes from their organic gardens? All so slim! Was no one in Marin overweight? They offered kindly suggestions: sage the place, put in skylights, tear out the bathroom, redo the kitchen, build a carport—and then they took off—they were walking the Camino, hiking the Alps, having lunch with a politician.

It was not that I missed Arkansas. My romance with the church bells and train whistles and fireflies and flowering dogwoods was over. I'd loved night swimming in Beaver Lake and the Scrabble games with the bluegrass musicians and the Sunday afternoons reading Shakespeare out loud; I'd enjoyed my students and befriended some of my colleagues. But I'd felt alone there. It wasn't home.

Weeks went by. I was busy, afloat, anxious, neither here nor there. Driving across the Golden Gate to the airport one afternoon, I reminded myself that I was exactly where I belonged, in the perfect center of my life: far out on the horizon to my right, my grandson Zack was banding burrowing owls on the Farallon Islands. To my left, in the hazy East Bay, my daughter Devon was arguing a case in a courtroom; behind me in the green hills of Sonoma my daughter Gretchen was writing articles for an organic farming magazine; and in the air above me Rachel and Annika were flying in for a visit from Amsterdam.

I'm home, so why does it still feel unreal?

Andy, the local painting contractor, sits down on his stepladder and tells me he is really a singer. He is taking lessons. He gives performances. Without waiting for me to ask, he takes off his paper cap, stands, fixes his eyes on the unfinished ceiling, and sings "Misty" in a heartbreaking, wavery, off-key tenor. He is so stoned his eyes fill with tears and I am so touched I almost cry too; only the sight of my visiting three-year-old granddaughter, droll little Grace, stifling a smile, stops me. I take Grace's hand and lead her out to the weedy backyard before she can hurt Andy's feelings. The wild blackberries are just beginning to ripen on the fence. I find two that are almost ready and hand Grace one and put the other on my tongue. We both squinch our eyes shut as the delicious sour seeds fill our mouths. From the house, Andy begins to wail "Moon River" and Grace's eyes pop open. "Where *are* we," she mutters.

I laugh and press her to my side. "Home," I tell her. "At last."

2014

Richard says his car is the next thing to go. He doesn't want to get stuck on the bridge, so can he borrow my Triple A card? He stands at the front door in a pair of coffee-stained khakis and a torn Ralph Lauren T-shirt, holding out my morning newspaper. I hesitate. Richard has been living in my basement for the last week. Everyone says I am crazy to let him stay here, but what can I do? He is penniless again and has nowhere else to go. If he can get over the bridge, I figure, he can at least start to look at the rentals Devon and I have found for him on Craigslist, the rentals we have agreed to pay for until his Social Security kicks in. But how can Richard go apartment hunting looking like a bum? "I'll bring it back this afternoon," he promises, taking the card.

Richard's car is a 1993 BMW. After it finally starts and I am sure he has driven away, I go downstairs to see how bad it is. The basement apartment is low and dark. When Gretchen lived here years ago, it was charming, with bright pillows and antique lamps and art books; a department store mannequin in a leopard skin bikini with a cigarette holder lolled in an armchair, and the ceiling was hung with Japanese lanterns. Used solely for storage now, the room seems crowded and claustrophobic. Richard has spread his sleeping bag on the mattress and set his synthesizer up by the window, along with his earphones: at least if he plays music down here, I won't have to hear it. His food is arranged on the counter by the sink: two boxes of pilaf, a cardboard canister of instant oatmeal, a plastic tub of cranberry juice, three jars of dry roasted peanuts, and four bags of Trader Joe's popcorn. I add the cans of Amy's chili I brought downstairs with me, open the drawer to make sure he has a can opener, and unpack the two sets of flowered china bowls and plates I no longer use. It's doable.

Still, his torn stained clothes bother me. Richard was always a careful dresser. In the afternoon I go shopping and, knowing I shouldn't, buy him two pairs of Dockers and three soft cotton shirts on sale. Once home, I phone Devon, who is pregnant with her third child, exhausted and tearful. "I'm afraid Dad will kill himself," she wails.

"Nonsense," I assure her. I have known Richard for forty-four years. He was depressed when I met him and he is no sadder now. Yes, he mis-invested heavily in his friend Jimmy's invention and lost all his savings; yes, he owes $57,000 in back taxes; yes, he was evicted from his last residence; and yes, he will have to file for bankruptcy. But he'll survive. He has always survived. *My* worries, I tell our beautiful daughter, are fourfold: (1) Richard will fall on the back stairs, hurt himself, and have to stay here forever; (2) he will fall on the stairs, hurt himself, and sue me; (3) I will fall on the stairs and need him to help me; and (4) I will fall on the stairs and die and he will keep the house.

"Mom," Devon breathes, "don't talk like that."

Richard doesn't return until late that evening. He raps at the kitchen window, making me jump, which makes him in turn chuckle. "Did you find a place to live today?" I ask through the window.

"A place to live?" Richard looks puzzled. "No." He hands the clothes I bought back to me through the open window. "You got the pant size wrong," he explains. "I take a 33 waist and anyway, babe, I do have clothes…"

"You do? Where? Where do you have decent clothes?"

"In storage, so I don't need these. But thanks, anyway. It was very sweet of you. And here's your AAA card back. It didn't work."

"What do you mean, it didn't work?"

"I don't know. The guy on the bridge wouldn't…"

"You broke down on the bridge?"

"Yeah, damn alternator, but don't worry, I know how to fix it."

"So, you never even looked for a place to live."

"No, but I've been thinking…the 49ers game is on tomorrow…"

"And you want to come upstairs and watch it on my television? No."

"It's a pretty important game…"

"Richard. I am writing a novel about a situation exactly like this. Only instead of just you, it's my dad and Ken and Mike who also move in here."

"Who's Mike?"

"It started off as a comedy. It's no longer a comedy."

"Mike is a comedian?"

"A musician."

Richard chuckles. "Oh babe," he says, his voice tender. "Not again."

I slam the window down.

He raps on the glass, grins. "That pretty set of china you put down there for me?" he says. "I *love* it!"

2015

Deborah and I still travel well together, probably because I don't care if she takes the best bed and she doesn't care if I take the window seat. We went to Turkey earlier this year and now she is trying to talk me into joining her at a knitting retreat on San Juan Island. "You need a break," she says.

I do. But a break spent knitting? I can barely cast on. My Aunt Jean used to snatch the needles out of my hands and whip the stitches on in a fury, and that was when I was a limber-fingered child and not an arthritic seventy-three-year-old. "Bring your laptop," Deborah suggests. "You don't have to spend the entire time knitting. You can walk. You can read. You can write. C'mon. It's a beautiful place."

It is. San Juan Island is in the middle of the Salish Sea and smells of salt and lavender fields. Our cabin is clean and comfortable, the forest lodge where we meet is gorgeous, the meals we are given are lavish, and the other participants—eight women and two men—are welcoming. The teacher is a sturdy nonstop talker who struts in front of us, knitting behind her back like the Jerry Lee Lewis of textiles; she wears a wig and cheerfully pulls garter-stitched falsies out of her front, the original "reconstructions" she's used since her mastectomy. She checks to see what we are all working on: Ilse is threading crystal beads onto a lacy shawl, Karin is making an angora coat, Pam is making a Fair Isle cardigan, Norm is making stocking caps with a mysterious motif he designed himself, Nancy is making a picnic blanket, Deborah is working on a pair of socks, and I have brought a sweater pattern I bought to knit for Devon's new daughter the last time I taught in Ireland. The teacher nods and smiles at each of us, then settles down cross-legged on the floor to show us a Mobius pattern she created. "Follow the river," she advises us merrily, "Don't cross where *you'd* cross, cross where *the river* wants to cross."

The others nod as if they know what she is talking about and, to my amazement, start to ape her movements. I try too, but I've no idea what I'm doing and at the end of the hour I furtively rip my mess out. Deborah is also stymied, but she has made a friend with one of the gifted knitters and goes off for some private tutoring before lunch. Lunch is corn chowder, caprese salad, soft warm olive oil bread with anchovy butter, and strawberry shortcake. I excuse myself after overeating and stumble back to our cabin and crash. When I wake up an hour later, I remember how much this retreat cost and decide I should at least start on the baby sweater.

The sweater goes well. By dinner, I have finished the back, though it seems awfully big for a baby, but then I come to the front. And the front features something called bobbles.

I study the instructions: K into front, back, and front again of next st, turn, P3, turn, sl 1K, K2tog, psso—okay. I can do it.

Only I can't. Not that evening, not the next morning, not the next afternoon. My eyes are bloodshot and I'm headachy and so furious at myself I am twisted inside, my guts an ugly skein of tangled twine. Unlike Deborah, who has mastered turning the heel on her sock, I have nothing to show. The yarn I've been struggling with is stained with my sweat. Knitting is too much like writing. Bad writing. I am sick to death of it. I am sick to death of myself. I brood about my life. I'm taking on far too many freelance editing jobs, teaching at too many conferences, and revising, still revising, the same tired novel. *All the Wrong Places* has just come out but even that hasn't been cause for celebration: my publisher has not submitted it to one single place for reviews nor distributed it to bookstores. They did finally list the collection on Amazon, but it appeared without a photo of the cover and had an Out Of Stock notice posted below the title. Out of Stock!

Norm, beside me at the dining room table, passes the platter of potatoes, risotto, pasta, and more olive oil bread and soothes, "Sweetie."

"Bobbles," I mutter.

"Don't do 'em. You don't need 'em. Sweater's for a baby, right? Babies just shove bobbles into their mouths and suck the hell out of 'em. Can't trust babies," Norm says.

I look at him with new respect and later catch him working on one of his mysterious caps. "What is that design you're making?" I ask.

"You can't tell? You live there. It's the Golden Gate Bridge."

An orange ladder with an S on one side and an F on the other.

"I sell these on Etsy," Norm says. "Made enough to come here."

"Oh," I say.

"Kidding," Norm says.

The sweater goes much faster without the bobbles and is just as cute. The only problem is the size: it seems way too big for a one-year-old. Maybe I'll save it and give it to Audrey when she turns three. At least I'm knitting it correctly. I sigh, set it aside, stretch, and go for a walk in the woods surrounding the lodge. Stepping into a grove, I startle a handsome red, black, and white fox, who trots away through a field of orange mushrooms, bright as poppies. How beautiful it is here! I look up at the fir trees and feel the quiet plunk of raindrops on my upturned face. For once I don't miss that someone I've never met. It's okay. I don't *need* to meet someone. My story collection *will* get read, my novel *will* get revised, the damn baby sweater *will* get finished. The river will cross where it wants to.

Or not.

The next day—the final day of the retreat—I realize that the pretty Irish pattern I have been following for the last three days is written in centimeters, not inches.

I will have to rip the whole thing out and start over.

I should be used to this.

2016

The drive to the city gets worse every week and today even the postcard views of bay, bridge, island, and sky can't make up for the traffic jam, everyone raging silently in their cars. Five minutes pass, six; it looks like I'll be late for therapy again. Last week Dr. J was writing a grocery list when I arrived and the week before she was looking out the window, her hands in her lap. Her expression as she turned to me was serene, expectant. "What shall we talk about today?" she asked.

She needn't ask, because for the three weeks I've been seeing her we always talk about the same things. The traffic! How stuck I feel, not just in traffic, in life. How depressed, pissed off, resentful, helpless, restless, guilty, worried, distrustful, scared, envious, lonely, bored, et cetera. Since I retired from teaching, I'm getting dotty. I sing "Hello, Dolly" to the cat, swear at the computer, apologize to the table when I bump my hip against it, yell at the television when Trump comes on, scold the toaster (*why did you burn that?*), weep over strangers' obituaries in the newspaper, laugh when a sliver of soap I'm trying to catch slips out of my hands in the bathroom sink (*it's playing with me!*), circle around my empty house hunting for wallet, cell phone, keys. My agent is about to give up trying to sell my novel, I'm drinking again—not much, just a glass of wine at night, but I can't trust that to last. I need something soon but I don't know what.

"You need a partner," Dr. J decides.

I shake my head. A partner is the last thing I need. I haven't had sex since the Texan and I don't miss it. The idea of someone underfoot all the time, hogging the television, adjusting the thermometer, crowding me in the kitchen, breathing next to me in bed? No.

"Someone intelligent," Dr. J muses. "Someone quick-witted and creative, maybe from New York…"

"You want me to have an affair with your husband?"

Dr. J doubles her pretty chin down, covers her mouth, and turns away. She hates letting me see her laugh.

"You're going to meet someone soon," Dr. J says. "I'm sure of it."

"Meeting someone isn't the problem," I say. "Liking someone I meet who likes me back is the problem."

"You'll be fine."

"Oh. Right. 'Just Be Myself,' right?"

"No!"

Her response is so explosive that I laugh. Dr. J looks surprised too and that makes me laugh again. She has never been this honest. "You don't think I should be myself?" I tease.

"No." She is serious.

"You think I should pretend to be pleasant, and cheerful, and…nice?"

"Why not? You are all those things, so why not show it."

"Because it's dull?"

"To you, maybe. Other people—men—wouldn't find it dull. You'd be surprised."

"Yes," I agree. "I would."

She studies me. "You're ready. Whether you know it or not, you're ready."

"For what, exactly?"

"For love."

Love? Even the word embarrasses me. I shake my head. "Too late."

"It's never too late," Dr. J says. "Trust me."

Driving home from our appointment, I scan the pedestrian walkway of the bridge, as I always do, on guard for potential jumpers: some solitary man or woman, hooded in the fog, lingering too long by one of the towers before dropping their purse or their wallet to climb over the railing. I dread seeing this, and with over two thousand jumpers to date, the odds that I might are not small. I've no idea how I would save someone perched on the edge; could I offer the same sort of panacea Dr. J holds out? I doubt it. I shudder, thinking of the bridge's slippery grids, inadequate barriers, its still uncompleted suicide net.

"Suicide magnet," my friend Michael once called it, Michael who claimed he heard voices insisting he stop the car and jump, Michael who needed biofeedback therapy in order to simply drive to work. I think of Dr. K's patient, Chris, that sad boy, and my friend's son Jay, that brilliant newspaper editor, and Heidi's bedridden father, crippled at forty. I remember the horror stories of the man who threw his three-year-old daughter over before jumping himself and the woman who leapt with her dog in her arms. Leapt. I puzzle this. Does anyone actually leap? Jump up and out into the empty air with their arms spread wide? I doubt it; I think people dangle, and kick, then drop for an endless four seconds, then hit the water 200 feet below as if hitting cement. A hard way to die. And why? "L'appel du vide" the French call it: the call of the void. I am not sure that this is a feeling sweet, kind Dr. J knows anything about, and as the fog swirls around me, full of its ghosts, I shudder again.

2017

January

San Miguel de Allende. Purple hibiscus. Russian olive trees. Swallows. Roosters. Dogs barking, trumpets blaring, church bells banging. Pink stucco houses half hidden behind gated gardens. Old women begging on curbs. Young men break-dancing to boom boxes in the zocalo. Clumps of middle-aged and elderly Canadians and Americans chatting in English over pottery displays in the Artisans' Market. I have come here to finish *The Home for Unwed Husbands* for the last and final time, and determined to do so, sit down in my rented hacienda, open my laptop, and immediately proceed to check my emails, my Match.com account, my OKCupid account, the ads for Nordstrom's, the menus of various local restaurants, the temperatures in Woodacre, Fayetteville, Seattle, New York, Istanbul, and London. Remembering the guy with the disarming smile I met at Judy's class reunion last summer, I open Facebook as well, just to see if he's on it.

He is. His name is Ralph, he grew up, as I did, in Mill Valley, he's a retired teacher, a widower, and apparently took his glasses off for his cover photo. Boldly I friend him, close the laptop, and take a nap.

The following day, elated to see that he has friended me back, I take another nap.

The next day I see he has friended me twice more and my heart sinks, for this means he's been hacked—he probably never remembered me in the first place. Why would he? We only met that one weekend. Well. Better let him know someone has gotten into his account. I send him a message and take a nap.

The following day Ralph messages thanks and how about lunch after I get back.

Lunch! I open my manuscript to Chapter One and get to work.

February

I am sitting with Ralph on the veranda at Cavallo Point in the Golden Gate Recreational Area—my suggestion for where to meet—and Ralph is pleased, since he's never been here before. He likes going places he's never been before, and since he's been to so many places, I'm glad I was able to please him. He gestures toward the view of bay and bridge and asks if I like sailing.

I consider my answer. "I like being on a boat. But I don't know how to actually sail."

"Have you ever gone under the bridge?"

A memory of sailing under it once with an English novelist whose dog liked me more than he did prompts another considered answer, this one a lie: "No."

"We'll have to go sometime."

Ralph says nothing more about sailing, but I learn about his childhood, his dyslexia, his swimming medals, his stint in the Navy, his time in Kenya in the Peace Corps, his PhD, his career in school administration, and his first years of retirement spent living on a boat in the Caribbean. He's three years older than me, born under the sign of Leo, an only child. He was married for over forty years to a Russian woman who passed away seven years ago. They had no children. He owns a small house in San Francisco and recently broke up with a woman who was horrified when he confessed to occasionally having suicidal thoughts…

"Really?" I interrupt. "I can't go near a cliff without wanting to throw myself over the edge"—a blurt which elicits a pause and then a polite nod from Ralph. He wears hearing aids and may not have heard me.

To continue…he is currently seeing a left-wing journalist from Berkeley who used to write exposés on the Black Panthers. Last year he went on a swim trek to the Greek Islands and a dive trip to Nicaragua. He is about to leave in a few weeks to visit old friends in New Zealand….

"Alone?"

He nods.

…and later this summer he is going to swim Lake Zurich with a woman he met on that swim trek in Greece.

We order our hamburgers—his rare, mine medium—and eat them slowly in the pale winter sunshine. I pick a potato chip off my lip as I listen to Ralph's deep slow voice, my eyes drifting past him to the bridge, which shines long and lean in the distance. He says "you know" and "things like that" a lot, and he hasn't asked me a single question about myself. He is shorter than I am, has capped teeth and flat feet, but he has nice hands, broad shoulders, a full head of silver hair, warm brown eyes, and that wide open trusting smile, like a three-year-old's. He is, I realize, nice. A nice man. I decide to ask him a question I failed to ask Dan, Richard, Ken, or Mike.

"Have you ever declared bankruptcy?"

Ralph blinks. "No. Why?"

"Just curious."

When it's time to go, we shake hands, agree it was fun, and walk off toward our cars in different directions. I don't look back and I'm sure he doesn't either; it was a pleasant lunch but there was no spark, and anyway, he's dating someone else. There's no need to ever see him again and I probably won't. But still. That smile. I drive away smiling myself.

March

Gretchen has been invaluable in planning my 75th birthday party and I am so grateful to her. She is everywhere among the guests, meeting and greeting, happily in charge, grateful to me for "letting her do her thing"—letting her! I would never have been able to hire this terrific taco truck or set up the tables and chairs or arrange the flowers without her sunny assistance. I am beyond grateful. The party has spilled out of the house onto the back deck, into the lawn, down to the creek. Devon glides through the crowd like Lady Madonna, Audrey in her arms, Grace twirling a ribbon stick beside her, Gavin's sweet upturned face as I feed him a spoonful of guacamole. All my dearest friends are here. Leo has come, surrounded by colleagues and pals who also adore him; Judy is here, and Deborah and Anne; Ken is here, still leaning on a cane; Richard is here, cheerfully telling everyone that he and I should never have divorced; and to my quiet delight, Ralph has responded to my last-minute invitation and has arrived —without his girlfriend.

"He showed me a photo of her, though," Judy tells me later.

"The Berkeley journalist?"

"Some beautiful blonde sitting on a Palomino."

"You're kidding."

"He was showing that photo to everyone. He keeps it in his wallet."

"His wallet?"

"He said he's swimming Lake Zurich with her in August. Some race she asked him to go on?"

"Well yeah, he did mention he was…"

"You should see her. A goddess." Judy considers me. "You're not interested in Ralph, are you?"

I shrug. "Not really. You know. Sort of."

Among the gifts and birthday notes piled on the piano, I find Ralph's "I've enjoyed knowing you," written on a supermarket card with a sailboat on the cover. Enjoyed? Past tense? Well. No matter. I'm used to rejection letters. And I've enjoyed knowing him too. Sort of. I collapse in the after-party clutter and put my feet up as Gretchen and I tear into the last of the cake.

April

Thank God for cortisone: The epidural I got for my sciatica is getting me around Amsterdam just fine. I lag a half block or so behind Rachel and Gretchen, but their laughter carries to me as I lean over the rails to look at the swans and mallards in the green canals, and I feel blessed to hear it. Annika, sixteen and gorgeous, keeps me company when we tour the tulip gardens of Keukenhof, and when we get home, Kai, twelve and twinkly, shows me his pet lizard Mystery, so named because she hides in the terrarium and no one can find her.

We sightsee every day; Rachel cooks fabulous vegetarian meals every night; and after dinner we sit on couches to watch old Jason Bourne movies—Rachel's partner Scott saying the lines before Matt Damon can. I knit, my daughters drink red wine, my grandchildren plow into the boxes of Goldfish crackers Gretchen and I brought them, and after the movies we all go upstairs and fall asleep to the sound of rain. This is my life as an Old Woman, I think, Mother and Grandmother, and it is a good life, and I am content. So why do I wake looking up at the high beamed ceiling of Annika's room, wondering if Ralph is awake too and if he ever thinks of me.

May

Ralph's sailboat is small and white and sweet as a dollop of vanilla ice cream; it's forty years old, named *The Rusalka* by his late wife, Russian for "mermaid," he tells me. Like all of Ralph's things, *The Rusaka* is both well-worn and well-cared for. I stow the sandwiches I bought and the cookies I made in the cabin and then, obedient, sit tight on the windward side as we head out under the cloudy sky. Accompanied by sea lions, coots, and cormorants, we aim toward Alcatraz and Angel Island before turning toward the Golden Gate. We are going to wish the bridge a happy birthday, for it is eighty years old today, but we never make it: the current is too strong, as are the winds. "Too bad," Ralph says, "we'll have to wait for its one-hundredth birthday." *We*, I think. I haven't heard that word in a long time.

"We won't be here in twenty years," I say, and then, catching Ralph's puzzled look, I add, "Or at least I won't. You'll probably still be around."

He will. At seventy-eight, Ralph is in terrific shape. I turn to look at the bridge before we tack. Up close like this, it's all struts and braces and crossbars, very male, practical, not mythical at all, not the bridge I've been romanticizing so naively. I realize I know nothing about the Golden Gate— not how it was named, nor who designed it, nor how long it took to construct, nor how much wire and steel and paint was needed in the construction. I could study these facts, but I'd forget. I stare up at the intricate underbelly of my old friend as we sail away, chastened. I have never known it at all.

On shore, Ralph walks me to my parked car. Feeling the sea still moving beneath my feet, I lean forward to give him a sisterly kiss goodbye on the cheek, lose my balance as his lips find mine, murmur, "I don't remember how to do this anymore," and stay in his arms as we continue laughing softly together.

June

I'm driving to meet Ralph for a sail and dinner at the Treasure Island Marina when Joni Mitchell's "The Circle Game," a song I've always loved, comes on the radio. I turn the volume up and sing along before it hits me that the familiar lyrics are telling me something I've been trying to ignore: time is running out.

If Ralph is surprised when, later, I mutter, "Oh what the hell," and let him draw me down to the narrow bunk after dinner, he doesn't show it. Nor does he seem to mind that we never sail that night.

July

And so I enter my Summer of Love. Fifty years too late but so what. There are no flowers in my hair and the only drugs I take are for my osteoarthritis. During the real summer of love, in 1967, I was married to Dan, nursing Rachel, and pushing Gretchen on a swing in the playground. Since then, Dan has died, sitting in his lounge chair in front of his enormous television in Santa Rosa, and I miss the flushed boy he was and the friendly work we did raising our daughters together. I wish he'd stopped smoking and taken better care of his health; I wish his life had been happier—but how do I know it wasn't? One of his friends has confided that Dan *had* been having an affair with his red-haired secretary in Sacramento, so I hadn't been wrong to suspect, and perhaps that was a happy time for him—I hope it was.

I do know that I am happy. Fragile. Buoyant. Hopeful. The summer days are wide and hot and full of light, the nights are deep and dark. Ralph is open and curious and kind and loving. He brings me roses, puts chocolates on my pillow, mows my lawn, fixes my front fence, charms my daughters, pets Paloma, wants to come to Kauai with me in November and to San Miguel de Allende when I teach there this winter and to Greece when I take my residence at the wonderfully named House of Literature next spring—he even, something no lover has ever done before—reads my books. I can't believe my good fortune. We sail on the Bay, visit friends on the Russian River, host dinner parties together. We go to ballets and operas and jazz concerts. When we walk arm in arm with our sunhats and our sticks, strangers smile and cars slow. Sometimes Ralph comes to my house, sometimes I drive to his. He loves that I have no agenda, don't want to get married, am not expecting anything.

"Well," I demur, "Death."

Ralph has survived bladder cancer and lymphoma; he has no truck with death. Driving across the bridge to his house, I imagine him listening to the news in his neat little kitchen as he chops mushrooms and onions and smooths out the recipe he is going to cook for me tonight. I like thinking of him setting the table with candles and flowers. I do not like thinking about him checking his phone yet again to make sure his flight information to Switzerland is correct.

For the only sour note in this summer's sweet symphony is Franzie, the young beauty who invited Ralph to partner with her in the Lake Zurich swim next month. I have finally seen the photo Judy warned me about and Franzie is indeed a goddess—tall, blonde, and statuesque—what does she want with an old man like Ralph? More importantly, what does he want with her? He doesn't know, he tells me; after all, he doesn't know her well, he just met her that once, on the swim trek to Greece. He's flattered she asked him to join her and set on going because he's never been to Switzerland, wants to swim the lake, and then, he shrugs, he'll just "see what happens."

What?

Looking genuinely, innocently confused, Ralph repeats it.

Enraged, I go to Dr. J. I am embarrassed to be so jealous and insecure but haven't I always been jealous and insecure? Dr. J advises me to let Ralph know how I feel.

So, since it seems I'm drinking again, after we've finished his delicious meal, I set down my wine and let him know that if anything "happens" between him and Franzie, I will be gone when he gets home.

Ralph flushes, rises from the table, and slaps his napkin down. "I don't," he says, "like ultimatums."

Tough. I don't like giving them. But that's that.

And that's how we leave it.

August

He misses me. He thought of me the whole time he and Franzie were swimming their eleven-hour marathon. The photo he sends of the two of them hugging triumphantly on the pier at the finish, both half drowned, and more than half naked, hurts, but the photo was taken, he assures me, by the Goddess's boyfriend. She has a boyfriend! Along with a Palomino, a red Alpha Romeo, and (she's a policewoman) a gun. She runs marathons, she skis, she cooks, she's amazing, but Ralph is not going to stay in Zurich with her. He wants to take a funicular through the Alps and visit a railway museum and the Einstein Museum and then he is coming home to me—and he is coming home three days early! And oh, by the way, he thinks I should know that a recently widowed friend from New Zealand named Antoinette will be arriving to stay in his house for two or three weeks when he returns but not to worry.

September

Antoinette's bedroom is right across the landing from Ralph's. They share the same bathroom. She is tall and handsome and vivacious, has been married three times before her last husband died, and she is not ready, she tells me, to "give up yet." She and Ralph go sailing and out to dinner.

I tell Dr. J that I'm too old for this. I'm drinking too much, eating too much, driving too much, writing not at all. My ribs are bruised, my crotch is sore. I'm subject to night sweats, diarrhea, constipation, insomnia, leg cramps, sciatica, and battering bouts of uncertainty. Being in love is hard for me. I don't think I can do it anymore.

Think of the bridge, Dr. J says. How it stays balanced.

How *does* it stay balanced?

October

Fire. The sky is sienna over the entire Bay Area and ash sprinkles onto the windshield. Communities to the north are in flames, all those vineyards, wineries, mansions, and trailer parks—Gretchen and her partner Dave may have to evacuate from Santa Rosa and come to Woodacre—they may have to bring Dan's widow with them. That's okay, I can hide out in the office I've rented in Sausalito. The office where I am supposedly putting "the final touches" on *The Home for Unwed Husbands*, even though it's long been apparent that the only "final touches" this poor novel needs can be met by a single match—or maybe by one of the fast-approaching wildfires.

I think of my mother waking me at midnight to drag me out to our big brick incinerator in Mill Valley to witness her throwing page after page of *her* second novel into the flames, weeping. What a fake she was, for I always knew she had carbons, but how brave she was too.

Richard likes to remind me of my mother's disappointments. "She should never have had children," Richard says. "And your poor father." He sighs. "Marrying a beauty and expecting it to last." I don't see Richard often anymore but in his odd, isolated way he seems to be doing all right, living in a duplex he can afford on his Social Security, practicing Bach on his electric keyboard, and dog sitting for Devon when she and her family take one of their frequent trips to Disneyland.

One afternoon I join him to watch our grandson's soccer game and while we are standing at the edge of the field, I tell him that I am seeing Ralph. Richard nods, unsurprised. "You need that," he says, his voice dismissive. And then, "How does Ralph get along with Paloma?"

November

Kauai. Ralph and I are spending a week in a friend's beautiful house just steps from the ocean, but I have ruined our vacation by slipping and crashing onto the marble bathroom floor in the middle of the night. I fractured my pelvis and had to go to the hospital: no ocean swimming or beach walking for me. I may not be healed for another six weeks. The friendly doctor on call, interested to hear that I am a writer, googles me after I leave the hospital and then phones, excited, to say that his son too was a Flannery O'Connor winner. I'm glad, and promise to order his son's book as soon as I get home. Ralph cooks for me, waits on me in bed, brings me gin and orange when I hobble in for dinner on my crutches. He pours red wine for me during dinner and offers rum over ice after dinner—I don't seem able to say No, but I better start, if I want to live—and I do want to live. He tells me he's never been so happy, but I imagine he's never been so bored either. He's brought his laptop and yesterday, while we sat on the porch, looking out at the waves, I urged him to write up some of the adventures he had during the years he spent living with his wife on a sailboat in the Caribbean. Obediently, he sat down at the kitchen counter and while I moved more words around in my terrible novel, he tapped out a wonderful short story about broken masts and pirates and sudden midnight squalls.

I wake up early the day we are to leave thinking that I too ought to write up an adventure or two from my past, but my "adventures" have been so mild! I am remembering my first time here, when Rachel invited me to walk the Napali Coast with her, and how honored I felt, and how I loved being with her in Kalalau. My beautiful twenty-one-year-old daughter, sitting cross-legged on a cliff, her long hair blowing behind her, gazing out at the ocean, listening to Mozart through her earphones. She had decided not to tell me that Kalalau was a nudist beach because she was afraid I wouldn't come, but my towel made a good cover-up, and after the second day I didn't bother.

Although I never went back to Kalalau, Ken came to Kauai with me several times later over the years, to hike and kayak, and I even came once with Mike, who followed another woman down the beach. But this time, with Ralph, despite my stupid accident and deplorable dependency, this time is the best. Hearing me think about him, Ralph wakes and snuggles against me and we listen to the surf and the doves and look out at the rain falling on the palm trees through the pale yellow-gray November sunrise, both of us content.

December

Ralph leaves for swim practice at dawn but I sleep on. When I awake there is a note on my pillow. "My love for you," he writes in his upright script, "gets stronger every day." I smile and put the note in the pocket of my overnight bag with the others; I don't throw any of Ralph's notes away; I may need them someday. When I am drooling in a wheel-chair, for instance, they will remind me of the happiness I'm feeling now. Who knows if our love will last? After all, the Swiss Goddess and he are still emailing each other. Antoi-nette threatens to return for another extended house stay, the Berkeley journalist needs him to help her fix her kitchen door, and a stunningly-beautiful-much-younger brunette from India who has graduate degrees from both Yale and Stanford has just invited him to lunch.

And then there's me. I am not trustworthy. I am impa-tient with Ralph's pauses, bored with his repetitions, often resentful about his need for affection and reassurance. I want far more time alone than I am getting. I miss my days of dawdling over my computer or walking the beaches or eating a bag of Fritos for dinner in front of the television, and I can feel myself cringe just a little when I hear his tires in my driveway. The ugly truth is that happy as I am, lucky as I feel, blessed as I know I am, I don't do Love well. I still have a lot to learn.

But I'm trying.

So, we'll see. I dress, and leaning on the banister, for my fractured pelvis still pains me, slowly step downstairs. Ralph has folded the *New York Times* to the crossword puzzle for me on the breakfast table and stocked his refrigerator with Half & Half. I pour a cup of coffee, finish the puzzle, go down to the basement, and snoop through his things. I've already found the hurt letter the journalist sent when he told her he was seeing me; I've read the carefully penned drafts of the breakup letter he wrote but never sent to the woman who didn't want to hear about his suicidal thoughts; and I've studied the hundreds of photos of his beautiful Russian wife. I've admired his many swim trophies and beamed back at his baby picture. I know enough not to touch his computer. (I'd get caught.) There isn't much else. Recipe books. Ralph has some great recipe books. I leave his den, careful to turn the light off before I gingerly haul myself back upstairs to the master bedroom.

The master bedroom is the best room in the house—large and airy with an enormous picture window that looks out over the city to the east and toward Marin County to the north. If I could fly, I could flap straight home.

But I like it here, in Ralph's cozy, clean, well-ordered house. I make our bed, find the pad of sticky notes, write my own uninspired but heartfelt *I love you too* and place it onto his pillow. If I leave now, before eight, I can use the day to get some writing done. I might even finish *The Home for Unwed Husbands*. Who knows. Miracles happen. I glance out the window once more. Two tall orange towers poke above the green swath of the park below; they remind me of the devil horns my sisters and I used to make over each other's heads in family photos. Hello, dear bridge. Escape route? Lifeline? Here I come.

2018

Not so fast. I'm still off-balance. I tip; I totter; I veer back and forth. Do I really want to "be with" someone—even someone as lovely as Ralph? I've been fine on my own for years. And is Ralph really so lovely? He's deaf, he's dyslexic, he falls asleep on the couch in front of movies I'm engrossed in. There's a whole harem of handsome women he has lunch and dinner with; he rhapsodizes about making love with his late wife on a boat in the Caribbean or in a tent on the Serengeti. When one of my friends asked him what he liked about me, he looked puzzled and finally said I was "fun." I'm not fun. I'm a cranky bitch. I don't like sharing the kitchen; I don't like sharing the bed; when he puts his arms around me at night, I feel so trapped I want to bite them. So why, when Ralph smiles or takes a plate I've just dropped and glues it back so perfectly that it looks new, do I want to fall to my knees and kiss his flat feet? Where do these waves of adoration come from? Followed so quickly by these little sinkholes of revulsion? Is this what having a relationship is all about? How do people stand it?

They must sway, like I do. They must stumble. I find I am stumbling more than usual at the San Miguel Writers' Conference. Ralph has come to Mexico with me but he is not happy. He doesn't like San Miguel; he doesn't like the clean streets and cute little stores; he has not come to shop, he snaps; he has not come to hang out with other gringos. He cuts me off with a curt "I know" whenever I point out something delightful, prompting me to drop his arm and totter off alone on the cobblestones.

It's a relief when the conference is over and we take a bus to Guanajuato, a town he approves of as being "more Mexican." We have a lovely time sitting under the trees in the park, eating ice cream cones, and watching children play in the fountains. We are perfectly, peacefully bored and it's fine.

But I stumble again in Greece. The little residence hotel is unchanged since I took my sabbatical there years ago; the same doves nesting in the same light fixtures in the halls, the same dove shit on the tiled floors, the same tattered flag flapping against the pole in front, the same walls blackened by old stove fires in the dilapidated kitchen. We climb the stairs to our room, push our twin beds together, buy a new shower curtain, a new rug, and thicker towels. Ralph protests when I rent the empty room next door to write in as well; he can be quiet, he says, I do not need to move. Oh, I think, but I do. Alone in that locked room I work on my novel, yes, but I also knit, nap, and do crosswords. He works too; he is researching a story about WWII. In the evenings we sit together with our gins by the narrow balcony overlooking the village below and compare our days; I do not mention the knitting, the nap, or the crosswords, and he tells me the news he has read in the *New York Times*. One article he knows I'll love is about a pilot who landed a plane in the middle of the ocean and saved everyone on board. His eyes twinkle. "A *woman* pilot!" he crows. Enraged, I smack my glass down, stand, and call him a sexist, which, wide-eyed, he counters by saying, Not true, he always encouraged the girls in his chemistry classes to succeed and it wasn't his fault if they chose to study interior decorating instead. *Interior decorating?* I hoot; he claps his hat on and walks out. Good! Go! Now I can finish writing my novel in peace. That's what I came to Greece for, to write, not to put up with the stupid prejudices of an ignorant old man. I stare at the white doves flying back and forth over the white houses below, until, at last, Ralph returns, and I, knowing I ought to mean it but not yet sure I do, apologize. He stays hurt and I stay apologizing for the next few days, until at last I do mean it. Ralph isn't a sexist. I know that. At least not much of one.

Next, Portugal. Having won a partial scholarship to a writing conference, I have come to Lisbon alone; Ralph will join me in a week. I am already in love with the city: the smell of burnt coffee, the whistle and grind of ongoing construction, the graffiti, the hills, the colorful tiles and terra-cotta roofs, the laundry drying on balconies. I figure out the trolley and the metro, only get lost a few times, and arrive for class early the first day, excited. I have forgotten how much I like being a student, how much I enjoy opening my notebook and setting my pen beside it; how good I am at simply sitting and waiting.

The room fills up with young people, pink hair, bare mid-riffs, amateur tattoos; then the instructor comes in. He's a writer I admire, a big guy with a big laugh, an ex-football player who walks with a cane, his baseball cap on back-wards. He is smart and funny and soon, I discover, mean. Granted, he is being challenged. The first story we read is about Bigfoot and the second is about a man who thinks he's a sperm whale. "It's Interspecies Day," the instructor crows. He leans forward, smiling evilly. "I do not find any of your characters interesting," he says to the first student. "I am not there. I do not want to be on this journey with you; I do not want to go to this place with you," he says to the second. He sits back, dimples. After class he calls me up to his desk to ask if I've ever heard of the Molly Giles who edited Amy Tan; yes, I sigh, I have.

The week progresses. I am here to learn and so I dutifully comment on the stories about zombies, robots, bad sex, and good drug trips. Dutifully too, I write down the instructor's advice, which is as well-intentioned and often as ridiculous as the stories: "Don't have anyone puke after their first kill." "Think of your novel's timeline as a clothesline and pillow-cases as chapters." "Stories are like puppies: you have to pick them up from the middle." I yawn and look out the window; I have no idea what I'm doing here. Yet the night before my own two stories are to be critiqued I am so nervous I can hardly sleep—I want approval. I want it badly. I want the young students to admire me, the instructor to be awed, I want an A.

I get an A-minus. The students don't understand my first story and they don't like the second one. One stern twenty-year-old circles every adverb with a purple marker, another suggests a better ending, another says the exact same thing happened to her. The instructor, blessedly, does understand my submissions; he calls me "a writer with mischief," gives me a few ideas, and suggests I send both stories out. I leave elated, despising myself.

I pick Ralph up at the airport and grin to see him emerge, brisk, worried, organized, taking over at once, steering me to the street, waving down the cab, giving the directions, which the cabdriver, from Angola, misunderstands, taking us instead to the waterfront, where I see for the first time the 25 de Abril Bridge that spans the Tejo River. It looks so like the Golden Gate in the summer fog that I unroll my window and lean forward. It has the same burnt orange color, the same graceful curves. "Look!" I point. "I know," Ralph says, not looking. "*Look*," I repeat, taking his face and twisting it roughly toward my window. He looks, nods, then blinds me with that crazy Ralph smile. "Hi there," he says. I melt.

We make it to the Airbnb, where he immediately falls asleep, worn out from his flight. He has put *Iron Shoes* on the nightstand beside him, and I notice that the bookmark is still where it was when I left home a week ago, on page 12. I look at his weary face, familiar and dear, touch it gently, and sigh. We probably have no business being together. And yet: for some reason, here he is. He hasn't left. Nor have I.

2019

No light, no heat, no phone, no Wi-Fi. This "enforced blackout" is for our own good, the utility company says; it will help deter the forest fires that are still raging to the north and south of the Bay Area—fires which were caused by faulty PG&E equipment in the first place—but not to worry, every precaution is being made to "keep everyone safe."

The cat and I are safe enough, but we are miserable. Paloma crouches in front of the dead heater vent, protesting in a relentless meow, and I pace through the cold dark rooms, muttering in my down coat, wincing every time a fire engine shrills by. What a terrible year. School shootings, mosque shootings, nightclub shootings, bombings, hurricanes, earthquakes, tornados, cyclones. Government shutdowns. Trump! Jeffrey Epstein! Harvey Weinstein! Devon with her MS scare, Rachel with her sarcoidosis, Bridget with her polymyalgia, Nora with her melanomas, Danny with his prostate problems, Deborah's right hand, DB's RA, Myra's wrist, Ken's gout, Steve's cancer, my own collapsed femur, shattered hip, high blood pressure, breathlessness. Toni is dying. Leo is dying. There's some new virus going around. My agent is tired of sending my novel out. I don't blame her; it's a mean-spirited book and does not deserve to be published.

Paloma spasms and throws up on the Persian rug. Paloma is a cross-eyed Siamese mix with a flower face and the gray striped tail of an alley cat. She is almost seventeen years old and should be killed. She shat in the hallway this morning, ignoring her litter box, and hid under the piano when I yelled at her. She has never been a nice cat—a show-off and an assassin—but lately she has been deliberately perverse, pee-ing and pooping on the floor wherever the fancy takes her. "It's just old age," the vet tells me, adding, blithely, "Cats aren't vindictive," which makes me wonder how he ever got his license.

I don't know what to do. I dread another dark night eating unrefrigerated leftovers and awaiting death by food poisoning, another dark morning shivering through another cold shower. Ralph wants me to come to his house, which is warm and cozy, but can I leave Paloma here?

"Bring her with you"—Ralph's latest text, generous as always.

I shake my head. Paloma won't like it; Ralph won't like it. I clean up the mess on the rug, hesitate, then pack cat food, litter bag, and litter box, and throw some clean jeans and sweaters into a bag. Carrying my laptop, two Jane Gardem novels, and a self-help book titled *Maybe You Should Talk to Someone* out to the car, I stop to assess the smoke in the air—it is gray and gritty and getting heavier by the minute. The driveway is littered with yellow leaves and the dangerous afternoon winds are starting to kick up again. I go back inside, pluck Paloma from the heating vent and dump her, yowling and scratching, into her carrier, then pause to look around before leaving and locking the door.

The exodus through Marin is orderly, slow, bumper to bumper. Traffic lights are out, streets are dark, schools, gas stations, and grocery stores are all closed. Paloma is silent in the back seat and I remember the many years she and I commuted back and forth to Arkansas—she was not silent then. After the tranquillizers wore off, she objected to every mile of the two-and-a-half-day trek and when her complaints grew so loud that I could no longer tune her out, I would lose it and start shouting "Shut up!"—a request so ridiculous that I often had to stop in the middle of Oklahoma or the Mojave and press my forehead to the steering wheel until I stopped laughing.

This dark afternoon, however, not a peep. Good. Maybe she suspects I would like to throw her out the window. We cross to the city with the other evacuees and enter another world: lights, music, open shops, and smokeless air. Ralph is warm and welcoming; his house is a haven of peace and order; we set a place on the kitchen floor for Paloma, leave her, and go out for wine and dinner. When we come back, she has made herself at home, and when I wake up in the morning she is contentedly sleeping at the end of our bed.

I bend over to pet her. So soft. So clean. Is it wrong to start every day saying "I love you" to a cat? I glance at the clock, lie back on the pillows, it's still early, not yet seven-thirty. Ralph has left to work on his boat; Paloma and I are alone. A pale strip of sunlight wavers on the ceiling, and I stretch an arm toward it. Maybe the fires have been put out at last. Maybe the year is going to get better. I think of Sardinia, the happy time I spent writing on the hotel terrace last summer while Ralph swam—and Venice, that golden week, admiring the floor tiles of the Guggenheim Museum more than the paintings on the walls, so afraid of falling again, but so glad to be there, and to be there with Ralph. I think of my new story collection, which has just won a prize. It hasn't been all bad, this year, it's had its moments.

I get up at last and, still stiff, hip and femur not yet healed, hobble to the bedroom window. It's a day dipped in tea, the sunlight sepia-colored by smoke. Mt. Tamalpais is almost invisible across the Bay and the towers of the bridge stick up through the haze like, like, well I don't know what they stick up like. Cat's ears? Paloma clumsily leaps off the bed, lands hard, shakes herself, trumpets an imperative, and leads the way downstairs; I follow.

2020

Gretchen says I'm nicer since I've been with Ralph. I think she's nicer too. Tonight, she is treating me to an early dinner and a one-act play in the city; Devon will join us. It will be just the three of us: a daughters' date. Feeling spoiled, lucky, and just a little wary, I slip into Gretchen's car, glad to see that she has kept the old dashboard doll. "Mr. Obama," she says fondly, patting it, and we both smile as our beloved ex-President, clutching his surfboard, starts to sway.

Gretchen drives like Dan did, alert, adept, quick to change lanes. We swiftly enter the traffic on the bridge, the city glowing white behind it. I am careful to say nothing as we approach the toll booths, although, as always, I can't help thinking about the time she crashed here. The booths still stand sentinel under the big round clock, but they have been abandoned for years. Everything is electronic now, I muse, faster, smoother—better? I don't know. I do know that the new road, which we exit the bridge upon, is better. It is wider, cleaner, far less dangerous. "Dad would have loved this," Gretchen says. "He hated the old Doyle Drive." I know she misses Dan; I do too. The Dan I miss is the boy who blew smoke rings and timed himself to drive the length of Park Presidio without hitting a red light; the one Gretchen misses is the well-dressed gentleman with impeccable manners who took her to elegant restaurants. "You're a good daughter," I say, remembering how Gretchen tended to Dan after his health failed, cooking, shopping, even decorating his Christmas trees, and how, since his death, she has dutifully, if sometimes resentfully, continued to look after her stepmother as well. "Thank you," she says, polite, curt.

We park at the Stockton Sutter garage, walk up the dark tunnel steps and into the afternoon sunlight. Our reservation is for five, but Bouche is not yet open, so we go to a little place next door, sit at the bar, and have a gin and tonic. It feels—there's no other way to say it—very grown up to be having a cocktail with my grown daughter, and I am as always impressed with the way Gretchen orders and settles herself at the counter. Alerted by the men around us who suddenly turn, we see Devon enter, tall and stunning in a sleeveless white blouse, her long hair curled upon her shoulders, her smile bright beneath her huge Italian sunglasses. So good, we all say, hugging, so good to see you, so good to be together. If only Rachel were here too! Gretchen and Devon quickly fall into laughing conversation, first at the bar and then later at the restaurant, not all of which—I am getting deafer by the day—I can hear, but I love watching them, these two beautiful strangers. I am aware of being a little shut down with both of them, not as relaxed or outspoken, not as funny as I am alone with my own friends, but they don't seem to care or notice, after all I am only The Mother, it's my role, and I won't be here much longer, and it really doesn't matter. I'm happy. I feel myself hovering over them like some useless invisible angel.

We link arms as we leave the restaurant, me, the shortest, in the middle, and head down the block toward the theater. I am still thinking about angels, and when a man behind us starts to talk about heaven, I turn to hear more, surprised when Devon quickly yanks me into a hotel doorway and Gretchen, just as quickly, flags down two passing tourists from Texas and asks them to escort us down the rest of the block. "That man had a hypodermic!" Devon hisses. "A what?" I ask. "A filthy infected needle," Gretchen snaps. Did they think he was going to jab me? OD me on heroin? Give me AIDS? Or this new disease, this thing Trump is calling the Chinese Virus?

"Didn't you see it?" they ask. No. I never saw a needle. All I saw was a pale fervent face in a black hood and I felt— interested. I let my daughters hustle me off the street and into the theater and I sit between them quietly as the performance begins, realizing, with astonishment, that I have become the child my children take care of.

2021

Vadim takes a puff off his cigarette, adjusts his white tennis visor, and sits down lightly in the deck chair his son Sasha has pulled out for him. Today is his ninetieth birthday. "I was born at ten in the morning," he announces.

"Oh," one of the guests asks, "and where was that? Odesa? Kyiv?"

"I don't remember," Vadim says.

The guest laughs but Vadim looks puzzled. It was not a joke. "My memory, you know…." He waves his cigarette in the air.

"Pops goes in and out," Sasha says.

"If you say so," Vadim mutters.

"I have trouble remembering things too," the guest says. "I have been thinking about the time we were both working at Ampex, Vadim, and you—"

"To tell the truth," Vadim interrupts, stubbing his cigarette out, "I have been thinking about Anton."

"Anton?"

"My good friend from Heidenau."

Ralph, interested, edges forward. Ralph is a Cold War history buff and he is fascinated by the past of his late wife's brother, especially his years monitoring missiles and working as a translator for the SALT treaty. "The work camp where you lived after the war?" Ralph prompts, but Vadim has turned to Sasha and raised his voice.

"Did Anton phone me today?"

"No, Pops."

"Are you sure?"

"Yes, Pops."

"My son hides things from me," Vadim says. "My son and his mother."

"No one named Anton has ever phoned you."

"You see?" He looks directly at me. Again, I am struck by the beauty of Vadim's blue eyes in his wasted face. With his tiny bent frame and white goatee, he looks like a wizard in a fairy tale. "You see how they treat me?" He raises his voice. "Ralph, I have been thinking about buying an Audi."

"You can't buy a car, Pops."

"I am talking to Ralph. Ralph, do you know what a good used Audi would cost?"

"You can't drive anymore, Pops. You had an accident. Your license has been revoked."

"I'm thinking maybe six, seven thousand?"

"Revoked, Pops."

Lyena comes out of the kitchen, sighs dramatically, and sets a plate of gray and green foods on the patio table. "Zakuski," Ralph the peacemaker says, picking the plate up and offering it to Vadim.

"What accident?" the guest asks.

Vadim pinches a salted mushroom, puts it back, shakes his head.

"Pops hit a motorcyclist last month."

"My god, is he all right?"

"He's still in the hospital," Sasha says. "We don't know yet. We're waiting to get the police report."

"You're not going to get the truth from the police," Vadim chuckles.

"Mom may lose her house."

"*My* house," Vadim corrects. "Did Masha phone?"

Lyena looks at Sasha and sighs again.

"Masha's been dead twenty years, Pops."

"But Masha never forgets my birthday."

I set down my untouched vodka and walk to the railing of the deck. It's an October afternoon high in the Oakland hills and the view is all gold and silver—I can barely see the distant bridge through the haze but I like knowing it's out there. I have been extra careful driving through the tunnels ever since Ralph told me about Vadim's accident. Vadim claims it wasn't his fault, that another car struck him and shoved him into the motorcyclist's lane. He says the video cameras never showed that other car because the video cameras have been tampered with. He says America is a treacherous country, no one is safe here, no one can be trusted...

Ralph's warm hand lands on my shoulder and together we watch the sun begin to set through the haze. We are not that much younger than Vadim. I want to ask him to promise that the two of us will not go out angry; that we will not end up paranoid and unreconciled. Ralph squeezes my shoulder in sympathy but then turns away because Vadim is talking about Heidenau, the time he and Anton hot-wired the night watchman's VW and tore out of the barracks toward town, the freedom they felt, oh that was the time, when they were free.

2022

It's been a year of arthritis and broken bones and broken teeth and hearing loss and macular degeneration. I'm falling apart and so is the house. When Ralph trudges up from the basement after fixing the furnace once again and says we both need a vacation, I agree.

We leave for Mexico City the day after the Supreme Court overturns Roe v. Wade. On the way to SFO, I tell Ralph about the time I stood with a placard outside the Washington County Courthouse back in Fayetteville. My friends and I were celebrating the 25th anniversary of that landmark decision, and while a few of the passing cars honked in support, most of the others waved their fists and called us killers. When I came home from teaching the next day, I was not surprised to see my front door had been kicked in. I wasn't frightened then, I tell him, but I am frightened now. The world is turning faster than I approve of, and in the wrong direction. School shootings and wildfires and riots. At least Covid is almost over.

We have only been in our hotel room two days, however, before we both get It. It's bad. I faint on the bathroom floor and bleed on the sheets and throw up and cramp over; I'm having trouble breathing, my head aches, I'm chilled, and I am thirstier than I've ever been. Lying in our huge bed I give myself over to thoughts of death. Of course, I have been thinking about death steadily ever since I turned eighty, but Mexico has embroidered those thoughts with scarlet and black, bleeding hearts and sugar skulls and thorn-crowned Jesuses dangling over altars of marigolds. I think about the terrifying gods we saw in the archeological museum our first afternoon here, their bulging eyes, open mouths; I think about Cortez, his sword dripping gore on the temple floors. I raise my head from the pillows. "We're never getting out of here," I predict.

Ralph calls a doctor.

I start to get better after the doctor comes, but Ralph gets worse. It's his second bout of Covid and while he insists it's a light case, he has a hacking cough and can't get out of bed. By the time I'm able to sit up, he is sleeping all day and I watch over him, glad for the chance to care for someone who has taken such good care of me.

I am sorry to miss seeing Mexico with him, though. We were going to eat in four-starred restaurants and tour the Reforma and poke through Freida Kahlo's house and catch the exhibit at the contemporary art museum. We were going to fly out to a coastal resort the last few days and sit on the beach and read.

Well, we can sit and read here. Our room in this old family-run hotel is wonderful. The desk clerk brings roses, the maid sets trays of food outside on the doorstep, our sheets and towels are freshened every day. We have carved wooden furniture and a corn-yellow bedspread. I keep the door open a crack so that I can hear the summer rain on the blue-and-white tiles outside and catch glimpses of the flower-filled courtyard; I befriend the oil painting on the wall. It's a desert scene at dawn, all rusts and charcoals, scrub and rock and distant mountains; no people, no animals. There is something timeless about the tranquil scene; it soothes me somehow, and I enter its desert for long minutes every day.

The days pass. Seven eight nine—"We've found a new way of being together," Ralph chirps weakly, and I laugh. By day ten, we decide we are well enough to go home. We trundle our suitcases over the tiles and wait for our Uber outside the locked gates of the hotel. It's four in the morning, dark under the leafy trees, but a few people are still out. Two men kiss on the corner. A worker whizzes by on a bike, two women click past in heels. The air is fresh and cool, quiet. *This* is Mexico City, I think. This is the moment I'll remember it by.

By the time we get back to SFO, exhausted, San Francisco seems foreign. We shiver in the fog getting into Ralph's car for the long drive back to Marin. I look out at the pale blue sky, the light sunshine, the gray bay glinting as we approach the bridge. The bridge itself looks different. What's wrong? I lean forward. Is the paint on the arches peeling? It looks bubbled, ugly, blistered. Swathes of zinc show under the orange. And the cables? Are they corroded? Construction equipment and porta potties clogging the walkways?

And those huge wooden spools of wire? What are they for? To hold everything up? The bridge, I realize, shocked, is *old*. It too is falling apart. I look out at the chilled radiant faces of the tourists posing for photographs against the guardrails and realize they think the bridge is fine. They don't see anything wrong. They know the structure will hold. It's just under construction, they know. Still in progress. Like us.

2023

Another stormy day in a cold dark house, and I want to apologize to my twenty-one-year-old granddaughter. Annika has come from Amsterdam hoping to hike and explore and meet other young people, but she has only seen the California sun a few times in the month since she arrived. She has seen other things—a pair of wood ducks paddling up the creek, a lone coyote trotting through the trees, a barn owl, a skunk, a racoon, five pregnant does, and recently, unfortunately, a huge black spider—the only creature she fears—on the ceiling. As I pace the kitchen, cursing the second power failure in two days and glaring at the unlit coffee maker, she laughs and points to a brown ball huddled outside in the rain—a drenched squirrel curled around its own tail. She has been feeding crumbs to a crow couple every morning; could she throw some Cheerios out to the squirrel?

Sure, of course, yes, why not. I have not said No to Nika yet; I have not had to. I love having her here. She has turned the downstairs apartment into a colorful boudoir with tapestries and plants and pillows and fairy lights; she has given me invaluable help with my computer, phone, and Spotify; she does the dishes and bakes pecan cookies. While she looks through the cupboards for extra pecans to throw out to the squirrel, I reach for my cane and clomp back through the gloom to my bedroom to get dressed. Since my fall on a Fairfax sidewalk last week, it's once again painful to pull on my jeans or tie my shoes. I cannot forgive myself for losing my balance so soon after my hip replacement and then for being unable to get up once I fell, for having to rely on the gallant drunk who hobbled out of Nave's to offer a stained sleeve to grip. I pull on a sweater and then, shivering, another. My phone is down and I can't reach Ralph, but he said to come anytime it got bad here. Annika is up for it; there's an open mic at a bar in the Mission she wants to check out, so I tell her fine, pack up your things, let's escape.

An hour later, she's ready. Nika is many things but a quick getaway artist she's not. I wait in the car with the heater on, skimming through Annie Ernaux's *Getting Lost*; I can't imagine anyone reading this book closely. *Why hasn't he called me why doesn't he love me*—on and on, worse than I've ever been at my sickest. Come on, Annie, I think, we've all had it bad, but you're positively terminal. I wonder how she ever won the Nobel for this kind of drivel and why my book club has chosen it. Her other books have to be better than this. The car rocks in the wind as I turn three pages at once; the storm is even worse now and we probably shouldn't be driving at all, but once Nika, breathless, stylish in thrift-store finds and immaculately made up, throws her pack in the back seat and settles down with a smile beside me, we splash our way out toward the freeway.

Nika says she likes the classical music station I keep on, but the storm is so loud I turn the radio off. Her own taste in music—at least what I've heard when we've cooked together in the kitchen—is blessedly retro; probably for my benefit, she's been streaming Bill Withers and Joni Mitchell—gentle stuff. Nika is a gentle girl, small-boned, with creamy skin and a brunette bob she styles herself with a razor. She has Dan's dark eyes and perfect elf ears and Rachel's long legs. The only signs she gives of the anxiety that often plagues her are the bald nubs of her fingertips, which she nibbles as trucks and cars screech past us.

I never bit my nails, but at her age, I tell her, I smoked. She makes a face and shakes her head. And I drank, and I was married, and I had a baby. She shakes her head again. "I don't want children," she says. She remembers how restless she was when she was a child, how terrible it was to have to hang around other children. She warned her ex-boyfriend that if he was looking for a family, he'd have to look elsewhere but luckily, he didn't want children either; none of her friends do; they haven't married or started families and don't plan to.

"And I worked," I add, perhaps a bit too pointedly. I have found Nika a small gig as a dog walker for some friends and enrolled her in a community college art class and a gym, but she's shown no interest in looking for a part-time job. I worry; she is bound to be bored living with just Ralph and me;

she doesn't drive and she will be staying another five months. What will she do with herself? She might meet someone who wants company on a road trip, she says; she'd like to see the country. She'll spend a few weekends with Gretchen and Devon and her father's sister in Oakland. As for her future, once she gets back to the Netherlands? Well, she'll probably continue living at home. She'll go to the university in the fall, but she's not sure she wants a degree or anything. She'd like to be a barista. Or apprentice to a tattoo artist.

It's my turn to shake my head. Both Nika's parents are hardworking professionals. Yet here's Nika, comfortably looking forward to a future of standing behind a counter making coffee drinks. And what about her brother Kai, who is failing chemistry and plans to celebrate his upcoming eighteenth birthday "getting wasted"? Perhaps ambition skips a generation? Or perhaps Nika and Kai's generation has lost the great gift of hope? And isn't that our fault? Isn't my generation to blame? But isn't her generation saner in some way? Better attuned to the earth and its needs? More realistic? Kinder, for sure. I could never have talked to an older person as naturally as Nika talks to me. I had too much shame. I could never accept myself as honestly as she accepts herself and others. I was a mess. But I was also lucky, I tell her: I always knew what I wanted to do with my life; I always knew I wanted to write.

Nika nods and points to her bag. "I brought your novel manuscript to read," she says.

"You did? Truly?" I gave Nika the manuscript a few days ago when she asked for it, but I never expected her to actually take it; I can't imagine she'll like it. She read constantly as a child but she only reads her phone now and when she picks up a book it's either nonfiction or fantasy. "I thought I could design a cover for you," she says.

"Wow!" I turn to beam at her. Nothing would make me happier. *The Home for Unwed Husbands* finally found acceptance last year, but my publisher has not yet come up with a single image for the cover; the book is due to come out in a few months and I have been fretting about it for weeks. Nika is a gifted artist. She does beautiful work. Wouldn't that be wonderful—to have my own grandchild illustrate my book?

"I'd love that," I crow as we start across the bridge. The rain is still slashing and I have to slow down. When the bridge railings start to scream in the wind, as they always do two-thirds of the way over, I hunker over the wheel; ever since an inept retrofit three years ago, the west railing shrills like a runaway truck. I'm used to the noise, but it still scares me; luckily Nika doesn't seem to notice.

"I would just love that," I repeat, once the scream fades behind us. We pass through the toll gate in the wide lane and enter the city in perfect harmony as the rain, as it always does once you get across, stops, and Nika says "Oh look," and points to a red-tailed hawk perched on a lamppost.

ACKNOWLEDGMENTS

I have been blessed with support from fellow writers all my life and this book would not have come about without close readings from my peers. I would especially like to thank Terese Svoboda, who saw most of these entries in rough form. The members of my Bay Area writing groups have been beyond helpful: Paul Bailiff, Rosaleen Bertolino, Kathy Ellison, Kathy Evans, Audrey Ferber, DB Finnegan, Tom Gartner, Betsy Imholz, Jonathan Krim, Susan Keller, Stevie Marlis, Marianne Rogoff. Thank you, all, and apologies to any I have neglected to cite.

Molly Giles was born in San Francisco. Her first collection of short stories, *Rough Translations*, which was based on her master's thesis (San Francisco State University), won the Flannery O'Connor Prize for Short Fiction. Four subsequent story collections—*Creek Walk*, *Bothered*, *All the Wrong Places*, and *Wife With Knife*, have also won awards, including the San Francisco Commonwealth Silver Medal for Fiction, the Spokane Short Fiction Award, and the Leapfrog Press Global Fiction Prize. She published her first novel, *Iron Shoes*, in 2000, and, twenty-three years later, published its sequel, *The Home for Unwed Husbands*. She taught creative writing for seventeen years at San Francisco State University and later taught for fourteen years at the University of Arkansas in Fayetteville, returning every semester break to drive back to her home in Woodacre, where she now resides. She has mentored and edited many talented writers, including the novelist Amy Tan, and she has led fiction workshops at Book Passage, the Community of Writers in Olympic Valley, and Page Street.